THE
ABSTRACT
WILD

A little too abstract, a little too wise,
It is time for us to kiss the Earth again.
— Robinson Jeffers

THE
ABSTRACT
WILD

Jack Turner

The University of Arizona Press

Tucson

The University of Arizona Press
© 1996 John S. Turner   All Rights Reserved
⊛ This book is printed on acid-free, archival-quality paper.
Manufactured in the United States of America
01   00   99   98   97   96   6   5   4   3   2   1
Library of Congress Cataloging-in-Publication Data
Turner, Jack, 1942–
The abstract wild / Jack Turner.
p.   cm.
Includes bibliographical references (p.   ).
ISBN 0-8165-1394-5 (cloth : alk. paper). — ISBN 0-8165-1699-5
(paper : alk. paper)
1. Nature.   2. Deep ecology—Philosophy.   I. Title.
QH81.T87   1996
508—dc20   96-10099
CIP

British Cataloguing-in-Publication Data
A catalogue record for this book is available from
the British Library.

In Memoriam
For Kathleen Thompson Turner,
who taught me to love poetry, painting, and music,
and Jesse Samuel Turner, who taught me to fish,
to shoot, and to love the wild.

Contents

Acknowledgments

✻

These essays were written during the past seven years. However, the events described, and the values expressed, are rooted in more than forty years of traveling to wild places in the United States, Canada, Asia, and South America. During that time many people provided various forms of support, encouragement, commentary on the essays, and fellowship in the wild. Hence my debts are numerous and often deep. It is said that we are born to our parents, but raised by our companions. I would like to thank the following companions:

Robert Aitken, Steve Ashley, Renée Askins, Dan Burgette, Judith Chase, Anne Stewart Cooper, Lyn Dalebout, Bob Dattila, Barbara Dean, Joanne Dornan, Rod Dornan, Huntley Ingalls, Martha Feagin, Alfredo Ferreros, Arthur Fine, Dennis Fisher, Jeff Foott, Micky Forbes, Nelson Foster, Simmie Freeman, Dr. Peter Hackett, Jim and Linda Harrison, Hannah Hinchman, Saeed Anwar Khan, Tom Lyon, Peter Matthiessen, Dick and Jay Moon, Ang Lakpa Moti, Gary Nabhan, Doug Peacock, Peter and Molly Phinney, Dr. Francis Raley, Dr. Jill Riegel, Dr. Gil Roberts, Kim Schmitz, Bob Schuster, Gary Snyder, Gerry and Imaging Spence, Emily Stevens, Susan Stone, Michelle Sullivan, Thekla Von Hagke, Brooke and Terry Tempest Williams, Rebecca Woods, and Lois Young.

In addition to her friendship and support, Susan Stone read all the essays as they appeared and added whatever grace and polish they have achieved. I remain forever grateful.

Allen Steck and Leo Le Bon of Mountain Travel, Inc., and Al

Read, Jim Sano, and Ann Aylwin of Geographic Expeditions, Inc., sent me to the ends of the earth for sixteen years and provided the finest days of my life.

Deborah Clow, of *Northern Lights,* where several of these essays first appeared, was a perfect editor.

Nancy Effinger and her staff at the Teton County Library in Jackson, Wyoming, were always helpful and forgiving. I would particularly like to thank the research librarian, Teri Krumdick, for tracking down every one of my often obscure requests.

I also wish to acknowledge the graduate faculty at the Susan Linn Sage School of Philosophy at Cornell University from 1966 to 1971, especially Jonathan Bennett, Arthur Fine, David Lyons, Norman Malcolm, David Sachs, and George Henrik Von Wright. Their joy in the life of the mind inspired others.

It is customary to say that the above are not responsible for either the content or presentation of the following work. In the case of these essays, such a statement would be too weak. My friends often strongly disagree with my ideas, and some, no doubt, are appalled. For better or for worse, the essays are my responsibility, my burden, my joy.

Introduction

✳

Thoreau said he was born just in the nick of time, and anyone who loves the wild earth today must concede we feel the same. We live with loss and rage, we write elegies and polemics, we remember a wilder nature — and that memory reigns over the present as an unrelenting and often indulgent nostalgia.

Surely we can defend the way nature was forty years ago with something more than advertisements for the good old days. But if this is true, we must address issues deeper than destroying wilderness, habitat, and biodiversity; we must do more than describe, again and again, devastating clear-cuts, species loss, or dangerous chemicals. We must examine processes at the heart of modernity that are only vaguely understood, however pernicious their consequences for the wild earth, processes that not only destroy the wild but diminish our experience of the wild.

The material impact of modernity on the wild earth is obvious and has spawned a powerful movement to protect what remains of wilderness and biodiversity. Like most people I know, I support this movement: I subscribe to the right publications and occasionally write a letter of outraged protest. I am primarily interested in another subject, however, and this book does not aim to further defend the value of wilderness or augment the vast literature documenting modern civilization's impact on the environment. For me, all that is axiomatic. Instead, I am concerned with preserving the authority of wild nature, or, more precisely, the authority of its presence in our experience and, hence, in the structure of our lives.

The antagonists in my story are not the usual fall guys—industrialists, ranchers, tourists, or loggers—though they personify the problem. No, my enemies are abstractions, abstractions that are rendering even the wild abstract. These include (1) our diminished personal experience of nature, the concomitant devaluation of that experience, and the attendant rise in mediated experience; (2) our preference for artifice, copy, simulation, and surrogate, for the engineered and the managed instead of the natural; (3) our increasing dependence on experts to control and manipulate a natural world we no longer know; (4) our addiction to economics, recreation, and amusement at the expense of other values; (5) the homogeneity that flattens not only biodiversity but cultural and linguistic diversity as Western thought, perception, production, and social structure spread across the globe; and (6) our increasing ignorance of what we have lost in sacrificing our several-million-year-old intimacy with the natural world.

These are more formidable opponents than cowboys or Republicans. Confronted with them, I see our effort to preserve wilderness and biodiversity as mere palliatives when what we need is a radical transformation that revalues the wild earth—its mystery, order, and essential harmony. More than a hundred years ago, in his essay "Walking," Thoreau noted that "We have to be told that the Greeks call the world Κόσμος, Beauty, or Order, but we do not see clearly why they did so." This is still true. The fight for the wild earth is a fight for the authority of that order, whether Κόσμος, Dharma, Tao, or wilderness; it is a fight against the deformation of the human Self under conditions of modernity more than a skirmish with some perceived Other; it is a fight that has barely begun.

The path to these essays was long. In 1973 a colleague stopped me outside my office at the University of Illinois in Chicago, handed me a copy of *Inquiry*, a then somewhat-obscure philosophical journal, and said, "Turner, you are the only person I can imagine who would possibly be interested in this. Naess has lost his marbles." The article marked for my inspection was "The Shallow and the Deep, Long-Range Ecology Movements: A Summary," by Arne Naess, a philosopher I knew mainly from his work in mathematical logic and as a fellow mountaineer famous for his first ascent of Tirich Mir, a 7,690-meter peak on the border of Pakistan and Afghanistan. I went into my office and read it twice. Then I looked out the narrow, tinted, unopenable windows of my office at the grid called Chicago and said, "I gotta get out of here."

I felt like Rilke confronted by the statue of Apollo and it saying to him, "You must change your life." I did change my life. Over the next few years I drifted out of academia and into the Himalayas; eventually I returned to Wyoming and a life of climbing and guiding. I have never regretted that change. I still view the world through the lens of Naess's brilliant essay and the ideas now associated with deep ecology, a new intellectual tradition best defined by the articles in George Sessions' recent collection, *Deep Ecology for the 21st Century*. That said, I must admit I don't read much in the literature of deep ecology because I find most of it dull.

My own perspective on wild nature derives from my experience there and time well spent with hunters, fishermen, naturalists, explorers, mountaineers, rangers, men and women from a variety of other cultures, artists, and wild animals. I have the glorious good fortune to live my year in "mixed" communities of humans, domestic animals, and wildlife. In the summer, elk, pronghorn, mule deer, black bear, moose, and eagles are a common presence. In the winter the same is true of javelina, Coues' whitetail deer, bobcats, doves, and vermilion flycatchers. Much to the horror of some of my friends, I even enjoy the presence of cows. Always there are coyotes and ravens, dogs and cats, and human beings who prefer the natural world—even compromised—to cities. At night the stars shine like crystal rivets in the blue-black sky. I would not ask for much more.

I have read the nature writer's canon—Thoreau, Muir, Marshal, Murie, Beston, Van Dyke, Leopold, Carson, Abbey, Shepard, Matthiessen, Dillard, Lopez, Nelson, Snyder—for most of my adult life. Recently, books by Diane Ackerman, Neil Evernden, and Robert Richardson have influenced my thinking. Most important have been the writings and thoughts of teachers and friends: Robert Aitken, Renée Askins, Frank Craighead, Nelson Foster, Jim Harrison, Hannah Hinchman, Tom Lyon, Gary Nabhan, Doug Peacock, Gary Snyder, and Terry Tempest Williams. Of considerably less importance for me has been the world of conservation biology, environmental journalism, environmental public policy, environmental politics, and the byzantine world of environmental philosophy—all elements, I believe, of "shallow" ecology.

Such is my tradition.

I wrote my first essay, *The Abstract Wild: A Rant*, when I was forty-six years old. Terry and Brooke Williams had dragged me from my cabin and made me swear on my copy of *Walden* in the presence of the Grand Teton that I would stop complaining and write. Tom Lyon kindly nursed it into print. Now the number of essays has grown—somewhat obsessively—without order or goal. That is fine by me. They are the work of a mountain climber who has had the good fortune to spend much of his adult life in wild places, often in the company of wild animals; they are driven by the anger and grief and elation of a man whose joy is inseparable from the continued existence of wild things, but who is as responsible as anyone for their destruction. Let me say clearly—*mea culpa.* And since these ruminations are influenced by my training in the Western philosophical tradition, let me say again, *mea culpa,* for I am suspicious of that tradition, its means and ends, yet I remain its servant.

I believe a saner relation to the natural world must end our servitude to modernity by creating new practices that alter our daily routines. I also believe that no resolution to the crises facing the wild earth will achieve more than a modicum of success without an integration of spiritual practice into our lives. Any spiritual tradition worthy of the name teaches the diminishment of desire, and it is desire in all its forms—simple greed, avarice, hoarding, the will to power, the will to truth, the rush of population growth, the craving for control—that fuels the destruction of our once-fair planet. I believe that virtually all problems are problems of scale, and I know, to the degree that I know anything, that desire usually drives us to adopt scales that are inappropriate to their subjects. This is as true for emotion and forestry as it is for hunting and global economics.

I cannot presume to objectivity—who can in this *fin de siecle* carnival called postmodernism? I have been charged with a belligerent ecological fundamentalism. This is true. But as far as I can see, no one has cornered the market on sweet reason, and the alternatives in my field of inquiry—traditional liberalism, feminism, scientific rationalism—are equally belligerent. Besides, I cherish the company of ecological fundamentalists who cannot abide the modern world. I cherish their rage, their rejection of the urban melee, their dogged undermining of the accepted order, their mistrust of technology and the applied sciences. If forced to choose between a presumed objectivity and my friends, God give me the strength to choose my friends—and may we prevail.

Yet, however fundamentalist, I am not pure—that is a practice for saints. I like that fine old Taoist saying: Water that is too pure contains no fish. I love my Ford 4×4 truck beyond reason, my Powerbook more so. I live in Goretex and Patagonia clothing, spend much of my time looking at animals through Zeiss binoculars, and keep in touch with fellow nature writers by fax and E-mail. I do not believe that modern convenience is incompatible with the preservation of the wild because I have a good deal of both in my life.

For me, a bigger problem is compassion. The plight of some loggers and ranchers, or the family with fifteen kids means little to me, even though I am committed to compassion. That *is* my failure. But as the Marine who helped raise me used to say, "Anyone who sees both sides of an issue doesn't see one damn thing." When push comes to shove, I know which side I'm on.

I am on the side of the grizzly sow and her two cubs in the south fork of Snowshoe Canyon; the mountain lion who tracked my favorite Escalante hollow; the raven cooing at me while I shave on my porch; the ticks that cling to me each spring when I climb Blacktail Butte; the Glover's silk moth fighting the window pane; the pack rat that lives in my sleeping cave on the saddle between the Grand and Middle Tetons and scurries across my sleeping bag at night; the wind roaring in the mountains; the persistent virus that knocked me down this winter; the crystalline light that greets me when I step outdoors; the starry sky. I see no need to apologize for my preferences any more than those who prefer modern urban culture apologize for their preferences. As Thoreau said, there are enough champions of civilization. What we need now is a culture that deeply loves the wild earth.

THE
ABSTRACT
WILD

1

The Maze and Aura

. . . a work of art opens a void, a moment of silence,
a question without answer, provokes a breach without
reconciliation where the world is forced to
question itself. — Michel Foucault

Just before dawn sometime in April 1964, I shoved my Kelty behind the seat of a small Piper Cub, climbed into the passenger seat, and fastened my safety belt as we motored onto the airport runway at Moab, Utah. Since it was empty, we kept going into the take-off without stopping and then climbed slowly, the little plane grinding for altitude. Soon we banked west, and as we cleared the cliffs bordering the Spanish Valley, a vast array of mesas spread before us, glowing faintly in the morning light.

We turned again, southwest, and set a course for Junction Butte, a landmark tower at the confluence of the Green and Colorado Rivers. Beyond the confluence was the Maze, a terra incognita some people wanted preserved as part of the newly proposed Canyonlands National Park. *National Geographic* magazine believed the Maze might harbor something to persuade Congress to include it in the new park. My friend Huntley Ingalls and I were to explore the area for three days and photograph what we found. The plane would drop us as close to the Maze as possible. In the darkness of the runway we had flipped a coin to see who would go in first, and I won.

The pilot—Bud—was silent. Since he knew the country below from landing at remote sites for uranium and oil companies, I tried to question him about features in the landscape. But the noise of the motor made conversation difficult so we lapsed into silence and flew on, bouncing like a boat in rapids off the thermals coming up from the canyons. Below, the Colorado River meandered through swells of slickrock muted by purple shadow, while to the north, miles of fluted red walls led to Grand View Point. By the time we crossed the Green River, the first light had illuminated the grass covering the sandbars, and pools of water in the slickrock gleamed like tiny silver mirrors. There was not a cloud in the sky—a perfect day.

At Junction Butte we had turned west toward Ekker Butte. Beneath it, to the south, was Horse Canyon, an open valley that receded into a labyrinth of slots—the Maze. On a bench between Ekker Butte and the canyon was an airfield that looked like a matchstick. Bud dropped the nose of the Piper Cub and we made a pass several hundred feet above the dirt strip. It had not been used in years, Bud said, and I believed him. It was covered with small plants and netted with arroyos. Worse, the south fork of Horse Canyon was far away, and since it led into the heart of the Maze, I feared that if we landed here, we'd never reach our main objective. So I began to search for options.

Beyond the nearest fork of Horse Canyon—the north fork—a two-track struck south to the edge of the south fork, a point now called the Maze Overlook. It was a perfect place to start from and I wanted to land there. Bud turned south. The road turned out to be old Caterpillar scrape, one blade wide—probably cut by a seismographic survey crew when oil companies explored this basin in the fifties. I asked Bud if he could land on the scrape. He wasn't sure. I wanted him to try. He was silent.

We dropped down for a closer look and banked slightly left above the narrow dirt path, Bud's face pressed against the window. Then we gained altitude and headed back, still in silence. Bud flipped switches and studied the instrument panel. Soon we were sinking toward the road, then slowly we settled in.

Several feet above the ground, a gust of wind blew us to the right and we landed hard in the blackbush flats. The right wheel hit first, and when the wheel strut punctured the floor between my feet, I pitched forward, striking my head against the instrument panel and spewing blood over the cockpit. The plane bounced gracefully into the air and Bud worked the stick, murmuring softly, "Whoa Baby, Whoa Baby." We lost control in slow motion, but we were without panic, a space I've encountered many times. Then the plane hit again, the wheels snagged a shallow arroyo, and we flipped upside down, sliding across the desert with a sickening screech.

When we stopped, we were hanging upside down from our seat belts. The pressure of our body weight made it difficult to release them so we hung there kicking, trying to brace ourselves against the windshield. I smelled my own blood—that strange metallic tang. I tried to smell gas, and all the while I'm thinking, "We're gonna get roasted." Finally Bud released his buckle and crashed into the windshield. He helped me release mine, and we sat together on the roof of the cockpit, trying to open the doors. Unfortunately, the wings were bent up just enough to prevent the doors from opening, so we both kicked hard on one door until something gave. Then we crawled out into the warm silence of a desert morning.

We were ecstatic—laughing, shaking hands, kicking our heels, and praising each other as though we had by sheer intelligence and talent achieved a magnificent goal. I licked the blood off my hands and congratulated myself for surviving my first airplane wreck. I was twenty-two years old.

While Bud searched for the first-aid kit, I got some water from the Kelty. I had six quarts, the standard rock climber's ration: two quarts per person per day, anywhere, under any conditions. We patched the gash in my head. Then, the adrenaline wearing off, we considered our plight. Bud felt he should walk to Anderson Bottom, a grassy stretch along the Green River with a line shack occupied by one of the local ranchers. I thought we should stay put. We had warm clothes, one sleeping bag, gas from the plane, matches for a brush fire, food, and water. Furthermore, we were highly visible—a light green airplane on a red desert. Within hours, Huntley would organize a rescue flight and easily spot us from above the airfield across the north fork. Bud would not stay, however, and after a few minutes he left, walking north with neither water nor supplies. The next day he was picked up near the Green River.

I examined my Kelty for what, typically, was not there: no compass, no maps, no tent, no stove, no binoculars, no flares, no signal mirror. This probably had something to do with being kicked out of Boy Scouts. There were just two climbing ropes, some rock-climbing gear, a bivouac tarp, a sleeping bag, a Leica M2, the usual climber's food—summer sausage, cheese, gorp—and water.

I walked to the rim of the south fork. It was perhaps five hundred feet to the bottom of Horse Canyon. Across the canyon were spires of shale topped by dollops of White Rim sandstone, a formation now called "the Chocolate Drops." The canyon walls were more eroded than the Navajo and Kayenta sandstone I was familiar with from Glen Canyon, but everywhere were braids of a real labyrinth. The so-called south fork divided into at least three more canyons and everything kept forking. To my delight I saw marshes and a pool of water. It was utterly still. I sat on the rim and asked a question that came up often during the next thirty years: Why, exactly, am I here?

I was there because of Huntley. During the fifties he worked in southern Utah for the Coast and Geodetic Survey, traveling by Jeep and foot throughout the canyonlands conducting magnetic surveys. During those years he photographed spires he thought would make interesting rock climbs and showed his slides to other climbers living in Boulder, Colorado. He had photographs of the Fisher Towers, Totem Pole, Spider Rock, Standing Rock, Castleton Tower, and the Six-Shooter Peaks. By 1964 these spires had been climbed, some by Yosemite climbers, but many by Huntley and Layton Kor. Huntley had published articles on the first ascents of the Fisher Tower and Standing Rock in *National Geographic,* and now they thought he might use his climbing expertise to explore the Maze. Since I had climbed a lot with Kor and Huntley, was interested in wild places and was Huntley's friend, here I was staring at the labyrinth.

The Utah desert was relatively unknown in the early sixties. In 1960 the road south of Blanding was dirt most of the way to Tuba City; the bridges were often one lane and made of wood. Eliot Porter's *Glen Canyon: The Place No One Knew* was not published until 1963, and Edward Abbey's *Desert Solitaire* did not come out until 1968. There were no guidebooks to these wild lands. Many of the parks and monuments and wilderness areas that now cover the area did not exist, and the country was vast and wild and easy to get lost in; there were no restrictions, and little management. We wandered the desert as we wished, lounged in the pools at Havasu, waded the Zion Narrows, climbed the desert towers, drifted down Glen Canyon, and explored the Escalante enjoying virtually no contact with other people. The Maze was simply another place on Huntley's long list of wild places to see.

Although the Maze was de facto wilderness, I did not then think of wilderness as a separate place needing preservation. The Wilderness Act was not passed until 1964. To the degree I even thought about preservation, I presumed it was conducted by nice old ladies in big cities. It certainly had nothing to do with me. I simply liked climbing big walls and spires and exploring remote places, preferably before anyone else did. Like most rock climbers, I didn't even like to hike. I didn't know the name of a single wildflower, and Huntley had to tell me, "These are cottonwoods" or "These are Utah juniper." My knowledge of animals derived mainly from hunting and killing them. (Years later, when I read Schopenhauer, I recognized myself in those days: "in the mind of a man who is filled with his own aims, the world appears as a beautiful landscape appears on the plan of a battlefield.")[1]

I walked back to the plane and wrote a message on the road with the heel of my boot: "All OK," "Bud" — then an arrow — and "Anderson Bottom." I drank a quart of water, pulled out my foam pad, and settled into the shade beside the fuselage. I had no books, no paints or nature guides. I wasn't worried, I was bored.

Around eleven in the morning I heard a plane and soon Huntley flew over in a Cessna 180 piloted by George Hubler, the owner of the Moab airport. After several passes to make sure I was ambulatory, they dropped a message saying they would land Huntley on the old airstrip. He would then cross the north fork and meet me at the wreck.

I settled back into the shade, even more bored. I could not get over the silence; it ate at me and I couldn't sit still. I wandered around looking for something interesting to do and found nothing. So I sat in the shade, oblivious to the glory that engulfed my every moment.

The day passed slowly with no sign of Huntley. In the evening I walked to the rim of the north fork of Horse Canyon and searched for him, but to no avail. That night I consumed more of my water supply. I slept fitfully.

The next morning, when there was still no sign of Huntley, I went back and walked the rim searching for him. Finally, in the late afternoon, I found him placing an expansion bolt several feet below the White Rim sandstone cap. He had already done some wild unroped climbing, but the cap was featureless, and that meant bolting. Soon he was up. We shook hands and greeted each other formally by last name, in the best British mountaineering tradition.

Huntley had left most of his gear at the bottom of the canyon while searching for a way through the cliffs. Since Hubler would return to the airfield the following day at noon, we had less than twenty-four hours to explore the Maze. We decided to leave Huntley's gear where it was and go on into the south fork. The plan was simple: we would walk into the Maze until dark, hike back through the night to the north fork, collect Huntley's things, and climb to the airfield to meet Hubler in the morning.

We returned to the wreck, gathered my gear, and after some scrambling and several rappels, reached the bottom of the canyon. After filling the water bottles at the algae-filled pool (we never treated water in those days), we hiked to the main canyon and up the middle of the three forks.

Soon Huntley began moving slowly and muttering about new boots. (Eventually he would lose all his toenails, which for years he kept in a small jar as a reminder.) After awhile he urged me to go on so I could cover as much ground as possible before dark. We dropped our packs in an obvious spot and I hurried up the canyon in fading light, moving rapidly, my eyes sweeping the landscape like radar. I missed the soaring walls and alcoves of the Escalante, the water, the seeps. I was still bored. But mostly from a sense of obligation, I walked on doggedly through the extraordinary silence.

Then, in the last light of day, I was startled by a line of dark torsos and a strange hand on a wall just above the canyon floor. I froze, rigid with fear. My usual mental categories of alive and not-alive became permeable. The painted figures stared at me, transmuted from mere stone as if by magic, and I stared back in terror.

After a few seconds, my body intervened with my mind, pulling it away from a gaze that engulfed me. The torsos became *just* pictures. My mind discovered a comfortable category for the original perception and the confusion passed. But strangely, seeing them as representations did not reduce the emotion I felt. I was chilled, shivering, though the air was warm. I could not override the feeling that the figures were looking at me, and that I was seeing what I wasn't supposed to see.

I can say now this fear resulted from confusion: perhaps from the exhaustion of the past two days, perhaps because of my anxiety for Huntley's situation and the increasing extremity of our position. But in retrospect, I believe it was the inherent power of the figures.

They were pictographs, but not the usual stick figures and crude animals I'd seen before. There were fifteen of them, painted a dark, almost indigo blue. Some were life-size, some smaller. Some were abstract, like mummies with big buggy eyes and horns. Others had feet and hands. One particularly beautiful figure I assumed was female. Among the figures were small animals, insects, snakes, and birds, all painted in remarkable detail. The most unusual figure displayed an enlarged hand with clearly articulated fingers; springing from the end of the middle finger was a fountain of what looked like blood—a spurting wound. Farther left along the wall were more figures. One did not appear abstract at all. It was dressed and masked, had feet, perhaps even moccasins, and held what looked like a spear.

I yelled for Huntley, hoping he would hear me and be able to see the figures before dark. In a few minutes he came hobbling up the canyon. Although he'd seen many examples of rock art throughout the canyon country, he had never seen anything like these figures, and he too was captured by their powerful presence. While photographing them with long time-exposures, we stared in silence. Although spooky and unsettling, they absorbed us, and we did not want to leave.

Reluctantly, we walked down canyon and collected my gear. By the time we headed for the north fork, it was dark, and Huntley kept walking into things and stubbing his painful toes. After a mile or so, we bivouacked, dividing up my clothes and sleeping bag and adopting fetal positions on a sandstone slab in the middle of the wash. Such nights pass slowly, like time in a hospital, where disturbed sleep confuses what is dream and what is real. I dreamed of traps and spears. Huntley talked in his sleep and screamed at nightmares.

At first light we were up and moving, eating gorp and summer sausage as we walked. By now Huntley was beyond cursing. We walked slowly, reaching his equipment by mid-morning. Then we climbed to the rim by way of a chimney that pierced the White Rim sandstone just below the airfield. Hubler arrived on time, hopping his Cessna over the arroyos, and soon we were back at Moab. We tried to drive home to Boulder, but after several hours we stopped to sleep on the bare ground under a cottonwood, my head resting on my folded hands. Then we drove on into the night, talking about the figures and making plans to return. I did not know then that when I returned—and I knew I would—it would be in another context, with expectations and knowledge that would erode their power.

The contrast between that long weekend and my job appalled me. I knew I wanted to have more experiences like that, even if I couldn't explain what "like that" meant. There was the adventure and the wilderness, of course, but what interested me was something more. Two months later we went back.

II

By May it was clear that the Maze would be left out of the new park, so *National Geographic* was no longer interested in our photographs. We were on our own.

Huntley and I had been talking up the Maze, showing pictures, and researching rock art, so numerous people were now interested in seeing the pictographs. There would be five of us on this trip. Besides Huntley and me, there was my wife Anne and our friends Judith and David. Since we wanted to stay for a week, the main problem was getting supplies into the Maze. None of us had four-wheel drive, so we decided on an airdrop.

By June we were back at the Moab airport. Hubler was piloting the Cessna. We removed the passenger door and seat, and I sat on the floor tied in with a climbing sling. It was going to be an airy ride. Huntley was in the back with a pile of Army duffel bags stuffed with camping supplies and canned food packed in crushed newspapers—there was not much freeze-dried food in those days.

The idea, again, was simple. We would drop into the south fork and sort of stall the plane while Huntley handed me duffels, and I would toss them out. Hubler said we would be close to the ground and moving so slowly they'd survive the fall. Having been a fighter pilot in Korea, he had the right spirit for such an enterprise.

An hour later we were above the Maze Overlook. The Piper Cub was gone, disassembled and hauled out to the old Colorado River crossing at Hite—no mean feat. As we dropped into the south fork, Hubler cut the engine back and we soared between the canyon walls, carving turns with the streambed as we lost altitude. When we were about forty feet above the ground, I shoved a duffel out the doorway and Hubler gunned the plane into what seemed like a ninety-degree turn, straight up the rock walls. From my choice view at the door I could almost pick plants as we cleared the cliffs.

Hubler was smiling and allowed that this was better than working for the oil companies. We came around and dropped in again, and this time I got several bags out. A third pass finished the task, and after dropping Huntley and me at the Ekker Butte landing strip, Hubler returned to Moab for the others. By midafternoon, we were all hiking into the south fork.

Most periods of bliss in life are forgotten, but our week in that wild canyon is an exception. The weather was flawless, with days of blue skies following one another like waves out of the sea. We explored all the south fork canyons, and David and Huntley descended the steep and isolated Jasper Canyon, which led directly to the Colorado River. Huntley found a perfect arrowhead. We sat in the sun, bathed in slickrock pools, dreamed of other explorations — and studied the pictographs.

The pictographs were still wonderful, but now they were just things we were visiting. I had become a tourist to my own experience. I tried unsuccessfully to recapture the magic of those first moments. I took notes, but they exceeded my power of description. I kept photographing, first in 35 mm, then with my 2¼ × 3¼ Zeiss. But what I sought could not be captured with photography or language. Indeed, the more we talked, described, and photographed, the more common they seemed. Everyone was appreciative, impressed, but the unmediated, the raw, and the unique was history.

I tried sitting with them alone in the dark, but they neither gazed at nor engulfed me now. The pictographs remained as they had for centuries, preserved by their isolation and the dry desert air, but what I would later learn to call their "aura" seemed to be gone.

When we returned to Boulder, Anne wrote a paper on the pictographs for an anthropology class and used my photographs as illustrations. That fall, Huntley returned with other friends for still another exploration, but then the Maze passed from our lives. I did not return for thirty-one years.

III

In the years that followed, my life diverged along an axis I came to understand as central to my life. Those early visits to the Maze, Glen Canyon, and the Escalante led me to the margins of the modern world, areas wild in the sense Thoreau meant when he said that in wildness is the preservation of the world: places where the land, the flora and fauna, the people, their culture, their language and arts were still ordered by energies and interests fundamentally their own, not by the homogenization and normalization of modern life.

After divorces and attempts at ordinary jobs, Judith, Huntley, and I drifted into Asia, not so much for adventure as for what existed only at the limits of our world: the archaic, wildness, a faintly criminal madness, drugs, passion, art, Eastern religion—the Other.

Huntley was the first to go. In 1965 he cashed in his retirement and with four thousand dollars headed east. He was gone two and a half years. His first letter came from Herat, Afghanistan, where he had spent most of a winter. The next was from India and concerned blue monkeys and a yogi with a master's degree in physics from Oxford who had taken a vow of silence and who spent his time playing classical Indian instruments. A year later an aerogram arrived from a hill town in northern India. Huntley had been traveling in Sri Lanka, India, and Nepal and was now living among a Gurdjieff group in a small bungalow overlooking the Himalayas.

By the time Huntley returned, I was in graduate school studying philosophy. We talked endlessly of his travels, of gurus, temples, Indian music, drugs, neurophysiology, Cantor sets, and Tibetans. I was envious. My life seemed small and I could not imagine how to make it larger.

Years passed. In 1974, Judith left for Asia. I was living on the southern coast of Crete for the summer, so we met in Istanbul and traveled down the western coast of Turkey and around to Side on the southern shore. Then we hugged good-bye. I rode the Orient Express back to Europe and flew home to Chicago to be a professor; she went overland, alone, to Nepal. Except for short periods, she has lived there ever since. She has a guru, she and her second husband were married in a Hindu ceremony, she studies with teachers of Tibetan Buddhism. Her photographs of Nepali craftsmen are in the Smithsonian Institution, and she has written a book on the indigenous crafts of Nepal. Several years ago, to celebrate her fiftieth birthday, she trekked for five weeks across northwestern Nepal with a porter. Then, worrying about his safety, she crossed the border alone and continued into western Tibet. She bathed naked in the sacred lake of Manasarowar and bowed to sacred Mount Kailas, believed by Hindus, Buddhists, and Jains to be the center of the universe. Judith's letters that first year further underlined my misery in Chicago and with academia, and I determined to go myself.

I spent the following summer wandering the Karakoram Himalaya and the Hindu Kush. By autumn I knew I would leave academia to see as much of the old world as I could before it was gone. Like the bear that went over the mountain, all I wanted to see was the other side, again and again. And I saw a lot. For the next eighteen years I traveled part of each year in the mountains of Pakistan, India, Nepal, Bhutan, China, Tibet, and Peru, scouting or guiding treks and easy mountaineering expeditions.

In retrospect, Judith and Huntley and I were part of a modern exodus of hundreds of thousands of Western people who left home and went to Asia. Some were hippies; some were pilgrims who ended up with Rajneesh in Poona, with Vipassana monks in the forests of Thailand, with Tibetan masters in Kathmandu, with Zen teachers in Kamakura; some were the first wave of what would become the adventure travel and ecotourism industries; some went to war in Vietnam; some went into the Peace Corps; some were merely ambassadors of capitalism and consumerism.

This great exodus and its consequences, especially the transformations of subjective experience that were both the end and means of many journeys to the East, remain unstudied and unknown. Some say, cynically, this is because everyone fried their brains with drugs. I think we still lack the language to describe why people went or what we found. This much, however, is clear: we dragged the modern world with us. We left home with a love of difference, but carried within us the seeds of homogeny. By the eighties it was over, and the cultures we loved were forever altered by modernity. We traveled a modern Asia that was no longer very Other.

My understanding of these events, and my own journey, is anchored in that early experience of those strange figures in the Maze—and in Walter Benjamin's justly famous essay, "The Work of Art in the Age of Mechanical Reproduction."[2] It began with a specific event.

I was standing in a meditation room at Hemis Monastery in Ladakh watching a German professor of Tibetology lecture his tour group. German-speaking members of other groups were attempting, with varying degrees of success, to translate his comments to their comrades. Behind him, two Tibetan monks faced a crowd of perhaps eighty Germans, Americans, French, and Japanese armed with cameras, flash units, camcorders, and tape players. The older monk wore a large white Pan Am button on the lapel of his maroon robe. The younger monk looked scared.

After a while it became clear that the high point of the professor's presentation would be the first public viewing of a particularly sacred *thangka,* a scroll painting on linen depicting a powerful Tibetan deity. Until that moment, it had been viewed just once a year in a religious ceremony attended only by the monks at Hemis. With a flourish the professor asked the senior monk to unveil the *thangka.* The senior monk turned to the young monk, and he froze. Then the professor yelled, the senior monk yelled, and the young monk finally removed a soiled silk veil. As the room exploded with flashes, motor drives, and camcorders, the young monk stood paralyzed, waiting for his blasphemy to be justly punished. But, of course, objectively, nothing happened. The professor smiled, everyone (including me) stretched their necks to see, and the earth continued to spin on its axis.

Later I thought of a passage in Benjamin's essay:

> The elk portrayed by the man of the Stone Age on the walls of his cave was an instrument of magic. He did expose it to his fellow men, but in the main it was meant for the spirits. Today the cult value would seem to demand that the work of art remain hidden. Certain statues of gods are accessible only to the priest in the cella; certain Madonnas remain covered nearly all year round; certain sculptures on medieval cathedrals are invisible to the spectator on ground level. With the emancipation of the various art practices from ritual go increasing opportunities for the exhibition of their products. (225)

What I observed that day in the Hemis Monastery was the passage of an object from ritual to exhibition. The object remained; I am sure it is still there today. But something changed that is reflected only in human experience, in, for example, the experience of that young monk. Similarly, the Maze and those wonderful pictographs remain, but for me something is lost, a quality of my experience of them, something Benjamin calls the "aura" of art and landscape: "its presence in time and space, its unique existence at the place where it happens to be" (220).

Benjamin's essay examines two of the processes that diminish aura, both "related to the increasing significance of the masses in contemporary life. Namely, the desire of contemporary masses to bring things 'closer' spatially and humanly, which is just as ardent as their bent toward overcoming the uniqueness of every reality by accepting its reproduction" (223). The primary mode of reproduction is photography; the primary means of bringing the natural and cultural worlds closer is mass tourism. The pictographs and the Maze started down this path when I yelled for Huntley, took photographs, researched rock art, and gave slide shows, and when I brought others there. Had we remained silent, others could have, for a while, shared that powerful experience. And what if everyone remained silent?

Benjamin also discusses the many ways that loss of aura affects an art object: it undermines authenticity, jeopardizes the object's authority, shatters tradition, diminishes the importance of ritual, and perhaps most important, "the quality of its presence is always depreciated" (221).[3] This last point is for me the heart of the matter. If I have an interest in preservation, it is in preserving the power of presence — of landscape, art, flora, and fauna. It is more complicated than merely preserving habitat and species, and one might suppose it is something that could be added on later, after we successfully preserve biodiversity, say. But no, it's the other way around: the loss of aura and presence is the main reason we are losing so much of the natural world.

Photographic reproduction and mass tourism are now commonplace and diminish a family of qualities broader than, though including, our experience of art: aura is affected, but so is wildness, spirit, enchantment, the sacred, holiness, magic, and soul. We understand these terms intuitively, but they evade definition, analysis, and measurement because they refer to our experience of the material world rather than the material world itself. Hence they are excluded from the rationalized discourse of preservation, and we are hard pressed to figure out how to keep them in the world of our experience. You will not read much about them in *Art Forum, Sierra,* or *Conservation Biology.*

Unfortunately, these qualities deserve as much, if not more, attention as the decline of wilderness and biodiversity, because the decline of the latter has its root cause in the decline of the former. We treat the natural world according to our experience of it. Without aura, wildness, magic, spirit, holiness, the sacred, and soul, we treat flora, fauna, art, and landscape as resources and amusement. Fun. Their importance is merely a function of current fashions in hobbies. Virtually all of southern Utah is now photographed and exhibited to the public, so much so that looking at photographs of arches or pictographs, reading a guide book, examining maps, receiving instructions on where to go, where to camp, what to expect, how to act—and being watched over the entire time by a cadre of rangers—is now the normal mode of experience. Most people know no other.

IV

In May of 1995 I returned to the Maze. Things had changed. The Maze is now part of Canyonlands National Park, and the pictographs that so moved me are no longer unknown. They have a name—the Harvest Site (or Bird Site)—and they are marked on topographic maps. A small library of books and articles describes, displays, compares, and analyzes each mark and figure, and various theories pigeonhole the paintings into categories created by these theories themselves. This doesn't mean we know much about them, however. Castleton, in the second volume of his encyclopedic *Petroglyphs and Pictographs of Utah,* concludes his discussion of the Barrier Canyon style, which includes the Harvest Site, with admirable candor: "The dearth of extensive archeological study of them makes it impossible to suggest the cultural affiliation or chronology of the style with any certainty" (289). Nonetheless, it is widely assumed that the paintings are the work of an archaic desert people, hunters and gatherers who occupied the Colorado Plateau from approximately 5500 B.C. until the time of Christ. It was their home in a sense we can no longer imagine.

The Maze itself is laced with trails all clearly marked on maps available at the ranger station, and the roads in and around it are described in detail by a series of books. Indeed, there is a hiking guide to virtually every canyon on the Colorado Plateau, a guide to every dirt road, another for every stretch of the Green and Colorado Rivers, and yet another to every river, creek, and stream in the state of Utah. Not to mention, of course, the rock-climbing guides or mountain-biking guides, or slot-canyon guides, or . . . And this is why southern Utah is no longer wild. Maps and guides destroy the wildness of a place just as surely as photography and mass tourism destroy the aura of art and nature. Indeed, the three together — knowledge (speaking generally), photography, and mass tourism — are the unholy trinity that destroys the mysteries of both art and nature.

The Maze is, however, by modern standards, still remote and difficult to reach — the standard approach is an eighty-mile excursion from the nearest paved road. The park describes it as "a rugged and wild area with remoteness and self-reliance the principal elements of the visitor experience." A visit requires a four-wheel-drive vehicle or a mountain bike, and a hard walk. The scrape where we crashed the plane is now the road to the Maze Overlook. At the end are two designated campsites and a parking lot. There's also a trail now, a difficult one that drops into the canyon and requires a bit of climbing.

To the degree that can be expected, the Maze is preserved and protected. In 1995 the park passed a tough backcountry management plan that limits both four-wheel-drive camping and hiking, and the rangers stationed there clearly love the place and guard it with a fierce devotion all too rare in the National Park Service. The pictographs remain unmarred.

I am thankful for all these things.

Enough history of the Maze is now known to place our little adventure in a historical context. We were not the first modern people to see the pictographs. Dean Brimhall, a journalist from Salt Lake City, photographed the Harvest Site in 1954 and later explored the intricacies of the south fork for other pictographs and petroglyphs. Local ranchers also knew about the site. Fortunately, I did not know any of this. Had I known the location of the paintings and seen Brimhall's photographs, there would have been less adventure, no exploration, and no aura — the "quality of its presence" would have been diminished if not erased. I can only wonder how many other gifts from the gods have been obscured by knowledge.

The man who visited the Maze in the spring of 1995 had also changed. I drove a 4×4 and played old Dylan and Emmylou tapes until I reached the infamous drop named the Flint Trail — a lovely so-called road requiring four-wheel drive, compound low, first gear, and lots of attention. For that I switched to Bach and Yo-Yo Ma. Spring had brought unusually heavy rains, and the desert was alive with lupine, globemallow, evening primrose, and little ruby clusters of Indian paintbrush. When I stopped and turned off the tape player, the silence was still there, but I was no longer bored.

I parked my truck and hiked into the south fork. From my pack hung a tag—my camping permit. I had reserved a spot by phone, paying for it with my Visa card and verifying my existence with lots of numbers. When I arrived at the Harvest Site, a couple was sitting in the shade of a cottonwood across from the pictographs. After we talked a few minutes, they asked if the paintings were the same as they were thirty-one years ago. When I said they were, the woman said she was glad to hear that. And I was glad to say so. To explain otherwise would have been too dark and sad.

After they left, I painted a small watercolor of the wall and figures, ate summer sausage, cheese, and gorp, and waited for dusk. Then I meditated with the figures for an hour, occasionally raising my eyes to study their mysterious visages. In the silence of the evening light, some of their presence returned. I saw the figures as a work of art, a group portrait—the shaman, the goddess, the hunter, the gatherers, an extended family including the birds and snakes and rabbits and insects. Perhaps the little band returned each year to this place and, as animals do, marked their territory. Whoever they were, they knew how to express and present something we have lost. At the end of my meditation I thanked them and bowed to them.

I am pleased the Harvest Site is preserved in the Maze District of Canyonlands National Park. I am happier still that the pictographs remain difficult to visit. I am delighted they remain in such good condition. I support the tough new backcountry management plan. I praise the rangers for their courage, their vision, and their devotion to a place I love.

But I wish we were wise enough to preserve something more. I wish that children seven generations from now could wander into an unknown canyon and receive at dusk the energy captured by a now-forgotten but empowered people. I wish these children could endure their gaze and, if only for a moment, bask in the aura of their gift.

2

The Abstract Wild: A Rant

The tigers of wrath are
wiser than the horses of instruction.
— William Blake

✳

Mountains have many moods. Even under clear summer skies I require my clients to pack warm clothing, to be prepared for the worst. I am a climbing guide, and like all guides, I am a skeptic about mountain weather. We abide by a local adage: Only fools and newcomers predict the weather in the Tetons. If someone does not have the right equipment — a hat or a pair of warm pants — I send them to Orville's, a nearby army surplus store that sells cheap wool clothing. Once, however, I sent a client to Orville's for pants and he came back without them, although he did not reveal this until later, after the climb was well under way. Since he was ill-prepared for our venture, I was annoyed and said so. He replied that the only pants available at Orville's were old German army pants and he would not wear German army clothing.

My client was Jewish. He offered no further explanation, no list of principles; he expressed no hate. His decision was visceral, as private as the touch of fabric and skin.

His action suggested a code: if justice is impossible, honor the loss with acts of remembrance, acts that count for little in the world, but which, if sustained, might count for oneself, might shore up a portion of integrity. Refuse to forgive, cherish your anger, remind others. This code was old fashioned, even biblical.

I understood my client. His conviction opposes our tendency to tolerate everything, to accept, to forget, to forgive, to get on with life, to be realistic, to get over our losses. We accept living with nuclear weapons, toxic wastes, oil spills, rape, murder, starvation, smog, racism, teenage suicide, torture, mountains of garbage, genocide, dams, dead lakes, and the daily loss of species. Most of the time we don't even think about it.

I, too, abhor this tolerance for anything and everything. My client's refusal stems from the Holocaust. Mine started with the damming of the Colorado River's Glen Canyon and its tributaries, especially the Escalante River, and specifically Davis Gulch, which I visited twice in 1963 just before it was drowned by the waters of Lake Powell. Visitors now houseboat and water-ski hundreds of feet above places where I first experienced wilderness. It broke my heart then and I am still angry about it. I am angry that Wallace Stegner and Edward Abbey would boat around Lake Powell as guests of universities and the U.S. government. I am angry with friends who kayak and skin-dive its waters. I make a point of being nasty about it.

Some will find it obscene to mention the loss of six million people and the loss of one ecosystem in the same breath. I am not ignorant of the difference in magnitude, but I refuse to recognize a difference in causation. In the September 11, 1989, *High Country News* there is a picture of eleven severed mountains lion heads stacked in a pyramid at the base of a cottonwood. You can see the details of their faces. They are individuals. The association with death camps is involuntary. These are only eleven of the 250,000 wild predators killed by the U.S. government in 1987.[1] No one raised a voice to the Animal Damage Control division of the U.S. Department of Agriculture. These deaths, the Holocaust, the destruction of the rain forest, and the deaths of two million Cambodians have a common source, a source that deserves our scrutiny and anger but a source we do not quite comprehend. I think of it as a tendency toward homogeneity—a hatred of the Other— so common in modern times that it levels difference across many categories and scales.

It is now often said (ever since Wendell Berry stated it so clearly and forcefully) that our ecological crisis is a crisis of character, not a political or social crisis.[2] This said, we falter, for it remains unclear what, exactly, is the crisis of modern character and, since character is partly determined by culture, what, exactly, is the crisis of modern culture. This question is important for anyone who loves the natural world, but the answer will not be found in the writings of Thoreau, or Muir, or ecologists—deep or otherwise.

Whether we focus on homogeneity or character, I believe that anger is a clue. Anger, anguish, and anxiety are all related to the Latin *angere* (perhaps clearest in the German *angst*) and they retain the cognate senses of distress, suffering, affliction, vexation, grief, and oppression. The initial sense, interestingly, is one of constriction — narrow, tight, strangled, a choking — as in *angina,* a constriction in the heart that cuts off the vital life force of blood. Something like that is happening to us now — the cutting off of life force. When anger becomes extreme and allied to fervor, enthusiasm, and excitement, it becomes rage. To be enraged is to be so angry as to be maddened, distracted, lost in fury — a very unpleasant condition.

The Buddha's first noble truth affirms the union of anguish and life. The ninth precept of the boddhisattva is "No indulging in anger." Somewhere between anguish and no anger lies the path.

Although the ecological crisis appears new (because it is now "news"), it is not new; only the scale and form are new. We lost the wild bit by bit for ten thousand years and forgave each loss and then forgot. Now we face the final loss. Although no other crisis in human history can match it, our commentary is strangely muted and sad, as though catastrophe was happening *to* us, not caused *by* us. Even the most knowledgeable and enlightened continue to eat food soaked in herbicides, pesticides, and hormones; to wear plastic clothes (our beloved polyester); to buy Japanese, despite their annual slaughter of dolphins — all the while blathering on in abstract language about ecological crisis. This is denial, and behind denial is a rage, the most common emotion of my generation. But it is suppressed and we remain silent in the face of evil; indeed, most of us no longer believe in evil.

Why is this rage a silent rage, an impotent protest that doesn't extend beyond the confines of our private world? Why don't people speak out, why don't they *do* something? The courage and resistance shown by the Navajos at Big Mountain, by Polish workers, by blacks in South Africa, and, most extraordinarily, by Chinese students in Tiananmen Square makes much of the environmental protest in America seem shallow and ineffective in comparison. With the exception of a few members of Earth First!, Sea Shepherd, and Greenpeace, we are a nation of environmental cowards. Why? Because effective protest is grounded in anger, and we are not (consciously) angry. Anger nourishes hope and fuels rebellion, it presumes a judgment, presumes how things ought to be and aren't, presumes a caring. Emotion remains the best evidence of belief and value. Unfortunately, there is little connection between our emotions and the wild.

A recent conceit is that certain wild places and animals and forests are "sacred." We have forgotten that sacred is a social word and that "sacred for me" is as irrelevant as "legal for me." We often ignore aspects of our culture that are sacred because we do not distinguish between formal and popular religion. Our national parks are sacred, Disneyland is sacred, the location of President Kennedy's assassination is sacred. These pilgrimage sites are sacred because of the function of entertainment and tourism in our culture. In a commercial culture, the sacred will have a commercial base. For many people, nothing is more sacred than the Super Bowl.

We have also forgotten the relation between violence and the sacred, forgotten that the wars in Ireland, Palestine, and Kashmir are, in part, about sacred land. If you go to Mecca and blaspheme the Black Stone, the believers will feed you to the midges, piece by piece. Go to Yellowstone and destroy grizzlies and grizzly habitat, and the believers will dress up in bear costumes, sing songs, and sign petitions. This is charming, but it suggests no sense of blasphemy.

We fear our anger because it might lead us to do something illegal, thus threatening our freedoms. This fear is justified. Any effective form of resistance to public authority must of necessity become a felony; consider the recent history of spiking trees. In a sense, violence is a test of the sacred, a matter of what will or will not be defended when push comes to shove.

Historically, effective disobedience has been met with violence. At Amritsar, India, in 1919, the British slaughtered 379 nonviolent demonstrators in cold blood and wounded more than a thousand. In 1930 they murdered 70 more at Peshawar.[3] The nonviolent demonstrators who successfully resisted German attempts to teach Nazi ideology in Norwegian schools were sent to concentration camps. Remember Kent State? Earth First! is a broken dream, its leaders neutralized by legal blackmail.

Violence breeds violence. The cant of messianic humanism conceals our culture's highest command: Thou shalt not oppose control. To effectively protest the destruction of the earth, we will have to face these facts, surmount these fears, contest that control.

A sacred rage does just that. The belief, emotion, and action of the little old Christian lady arrested for protesting abortion can reasonably be connected to the sacred. So can the nonviolent protest of a Buddhist peace activist. So can the terrorist activities of a Moslem fanatic. Whether we like or dislike these acts, think them good or bad, right or wrong, is irrelevant to their being sacred. They are sacred because of their spiritual origin. For the believer, the sacred is the source of belief, emotion, and action, what is good and what is right; it *determines* life and is immune to merely secular legal and ethical judgments. This is vital religion, lived belief. Old forests will be sacred, and their destruction blasphemous, when we demonstrate that our rage is immune to secular judgment. The hard question is this: Do we *want* nature to be sacred? Can this be chosen? Should it be?

I am inclined to agree with Dōgen: "Truly nothing is sacred, hard as iron."[4] But this leaves me with my rage intact and a sense of impotence.

Effective protests are grounded in a refusal to accept what is normal. We accept a diminished world as normal; we accept a diminished way of life as normal; we accept diminished human beings as normal. What was once considered pathological becomes statistically common and eventually "normal"—a move that often veils denial. Decayed teeth are statistically common, just like smog and environmentally caused cancers. That a statistically common decayed tooth is also an abnormal tooth, a pathological tooth, a diminished tooth, a painful, horrible tooth, is a fact we deny. Until it is our tooth. At present most of us do not experience the loss of the wild like we experience a toothache. That is the problem. The "normal" wilderness—wilderness most people know—is a charade of areas, zones, and management plans that is driving the real wild into oblivion. We deny this, accepting the semblance instead of demanding the real. This, too, is normal; modern culture is increasingly a culture of semblance and simulacra.

Effective protests are grounded in an alternative vision. Unfortunately, we have no coherent vision of an alternative to our present maladies. Deep ecology does not, as yet, offer a coherent vision. Our main resource, Sessions and Devall's *Deep Ecology*, is a hodgepodge of lists, principles, declarations, quotations, clippings from every conceivable tradition, and tidbits of New Age kitsch. The authors do not clearly say what they mean, they do not forcefully argue for what they believe, they do not create anything new. Presented as revolutionary tracts aimed at subverting Western civilization, these writings on deep ecology should embarrass us with their intellectual timidity. Compare them with other revolutionary works—*Leviathan*, *The Social Contract*, the *Communist Manifesto*—or the critical thought of recent European thinkers such as Michael Foucault, Jürgen Habermas, or Anthony Giddens, and we glimpse the depth of our muddle. Deep ecology is suspicious. It lacks passion, an absence that is acutely disturbing given the current state of affairs. A reading of Marx's theses on Feuerbach is in order, especially the eleventh: "The philosophers have only *interpreted* the world, in various ways; the point, however, is to *change* it." [5] Can we change it? Do we care that much?

Apathy, complacency, docility, and cowardice are not new in America; they were, for instance, major subjects of both *Walden* and "Resistance to Civil Government." Thoreau, it is always helpful to recall, was for most of his life considered a maladjusted failure, even by those who knew and loved him (Muir, too, for that matter). But for the present let it be, at best, controversial and, at worst, improper to have strong moral feelings about the treatment of animals, plants, and places—an emotional mistake. Like being in love with the number two. Let the case for the destruction of the earth rest. We are smothered with facts. They are both depressing and endless. What is unsettling is that we are all so apathetic.

The social reasons for our apathy are numerous: religious traditions such as Christianity and Buddhism that glorify acceptance and condemn emotion (particularly anger) and judgment; a liberal ideology that extols relativism, pluralism, tolerance, and pragmatism in internal affairs; the inertia of any social structure; a claustrophobic conformity behind a mask of individualism; and a shortsighted and self-serving love of expediency. The most readily accepted social criticism in our society is cloaked in humor—the political cartoons of Gary Trudeau and Gary Larson, for example. Most of us don't talk of normal and abnormal or good and evil; we talk about what we like and dislike, as if discussing ice cream. Perhaps what I fear most is that the destruction of the natural world to serve human needs and ideals will become an issue decided by opinion polls and surveys that track the gentle undulations of the true, the good, and the beautiful among a people now ignorant of what was once their wild and beautiful home.

There are also private reasons for apathy and indifference. As Marcuse noted twenty-five years ago, "The intellectual and emotional refusal 'to go along' appears neurotic and impotent."[6] Even at the alleged high point of Western civilization, we are ridiculed for criticizing public pathology. Criticize the greed of the rich and you are *envious*. Become enraged at the killing of 100,000 dolphins every year and you are *infantile*. Protest the FBI's harassment of dissident organizations and you *have a problem with authority*. Condemn the state for exposing citizens to radiation from nuclear-arms testing and you are *unpatriotic*.

The reduction of social criticism to private defect is incessant in our culture; it cripples our outrage and numbs our moral imagination. Convinced that it is really *our* problem, we are no longer astonished by evil and living nightmares no longer awaken us. We are put down, so we shut up, abandoning the prospect of autonomy, self-respect, and integrity. Signing more petitions, giving money, or joining another environmental organization helps some, but these things are too abstract to help *us* and *our* problem. These means are too far removed from the end, the intention unachieved. Indeed, our apathy and cowardice stem, in part, from this: these abstractions *never* work, they *never* achieve a sense of power and fulfillment. They correct neither the cause nor the effect. We end up feeling helpless, and since it is human nature to want to avoid feeling helpless, we become dissociated, cynical, and depressed.

Better to live in the presence of the wild—feel it, smell it, see it—and do something real that succeeds, like Gary Nabhan's preservation of wild seeds or Doug Peacock's intimacy with grizzlies.[7] We know that in the end moral efficacy will manifest knowledge and love: our intimacies. We only value what we know and love, and we no longer know or love the wild. So instead we accept substitutes, imitations, semblances, and fakes—a diminished wild. We accept abstract information in place of personal experience and communication. This removes us from the true wild and severs our recognition of its value. Most people don't miss it and won't miss it in the future. Most people literally do not know what we are talking about.

To reverse this situation we must become so intimate with wild animals, with plants and places, that we answer to their destruction from the gut. Like when we discover the landlady strangling our cat.

If anything is endangered in America it is our experience of wild nature—gross contact. There is knowledge only the wild can give us, knowledge specific to the experience of it. These are its gifts to us. In this, wilderness is no different from music, painting, poetry, or love: you concede the abundance and try to respond with grace.

The problem is that we no longer know what these gifts are. In our effort to go beyond anthropocentric defenses of nature, to emphasize its intrinsic value and right to exist independently of us, we forget the reciprocity between the wild in nature and the wild in us, between knowledge of the wild and knowledge of the self that was central to all primitive cultures. Once the meaning of the wild is forgotten, because the relevant experience is lost, we abuse the word, literally, mis-use it. The savagery and brutality of gang rape is now called "wilding," and in New Age retreats men search for a "wild man within" by sitting in the mud beating drums.

Why do we associate the savage, the brutal, with the wild? The savagery of nature fades to nothing compared to the savagery of human agency. The most civilized nations on the planet killed sixty to seventy million of each other's citizens in the thirty-year span from the beginning of World War I to the end of World War II. Dante, Shakespeare, Goethe, Kant, Rousseau, Dōgen, Mill, Beethoven, Bach, Mozart, Manet, Basho, Van Gogh, and Hokusai didn't make any difference. The rule of law, human rights, democracy, the sovereignty of nations, liberal education, scientific method, and the presence of an Emperor God didn't make any difference. Protestantism, Catholicism, Greek and Russian Orthodoxy, Buddhism, Shintoism, and Islam didn't make any difference. How can we, at this time in history, think of a grizzly or a wolf as . . . savage? Why laugh at the idea of the noble savage when we have discovered no savage more savage than civilized man?

The easiest way to experience a bit of what the wild was like is to go into a great forest at night alone. Sit quietly for awhile. Something very old will return. It is well described by Ortega y Gasset in *Meditations on Hunting:* "The hunter . . . needs to prepare an attention which does not consist in riveting itself on the presumed but consists precisely in not assuming anything and in avoiding inattentiveness. It is a 'universal' attention, which does not inscribe itself on any point and tries to be on all points" (130).

This is similar to certain meditation techniques, especially "shikantaza," a practice of the Soto sect of Zen. It is not an accident that Lama Govinda believed meditation arose among the hunting cultures of the Himalayan foothills; it is not an accident that the Balti and the Golok tribes of the Himalaya handle utensils like masters of the tea ceremony. Alone in the natural world, time is less dense, less filled with information; space is close; smell and hearing and touch reassert themselves. The wild is keenly sensual. In a true wilderness we are like that much of the time, even in broad daylight. Alert, careful, literally "full of care." Not because of principles, but because of something very old.

The majority of Americans no longer know this experience of the wild. We are surrounded by national parks, wilderness areas, wildlife preserves, sanctuaries, and refuges. We love to visit them. We also visit foreign parks and wilderness; we visit wild, exotic cultures. We are deluged with commercial images of wildness: coffee-table books, calendars, postcards, posters, T-shirts, and place mats. There are nature movies, a comprehensive bibliography of nature books would strain a computer, and hundreds of nature magazines with every conceivable emphasis: yuppie outdoor magazines, geographical magazines, philosophical magazines, scientific magazines, ecology magazines, political magazines. Zoos and animal parks and marine lands abound, displaying a selection of beasts exceeded only by Noah's.

From this we conclude that modern man's knowledge and experience of wild nature is extensive. But it is not. Rather, what we have is extensive experience of a severely diminished wilderness animal or place—a caricature of its former self. Or we have extensive indirect experience of wild nature mediated via photographic images and the written word. But this is not experience of the wild, not gross contact.

The national parks were created for, and by, tourism, and they emphasize what interests a tourist—the picturesque and the odd. They are managed with two ends in mind: entertainment and preservation of the resource base for entertainment. Most visitors rarely leave their cars except to eat, sleep, or go to the john. In Grand Teton National Park, 93 percent of the visitors never visit the backcountry. If visitors do make other stops, it is at designated picturesque "scenes" or educational exhibits presenting amusing facts—the names of peaks, a bit of history—or, very occasionally, for passive recreation, a ride in a boat or an organized nature walk.

None of this is accidental. It results from carefully crafted management plans that channel the flow of tourists according to maximum utility — utility defined by the ends of entertainment, efficiency, and resource preservation.

The problem is not what people do in the parks, but what they are discouraged or prevented from doing. No one, for instance, is encouraged to climb mountains, backpack, or canoe alone. Hikers are discouraged from traveling off trail, especially in unpatrolled areas with difficult rescue. We are often prohibited from visiting remote areas where we might encounter bears. Our movements are always subjected to what Foucault calls "normalizing surveillance." There are traffic police, climbing police, river police, and backcountry police. They carry guns and Mace, wear bullet-proof vests, and levy fines. It is *illegal* to wander around the national parks without a permit defining where you go and where you stay and how long you stay. In every manner conceivable, national parks separate us from the freedom that is the promise of the wild.

If we go into a designated wilderness area, say the Bridger-Teton Wilderness in Wyoming, we are slightly less restricted, but we find as much degradation of the wild environment. We see signs and hike horse trails and cross sturdy bridges and find maps on large boards at trail junctions. We meet patrolling rangers, Boy Scout and Girl Scout troops working on character, and an Outward Bound course teaching wilderness skills in a corporate-management seminar. We meet trail crews, pack trains, and hikers galore. At night we see the distant lights of cities and highways and sodium-vapor lamps in the yards of farms and ranches. Satellites pass overhead. By day, contrails from commercial jets mar the sky, and military planes, private jets, small aircraft, and helicopters shatter any calm. (I have been flattened by military jets moving at supersonic speeds just above the desert in a designated wilderness area in Organ Pipe National Monument.) We camp by a lake, the outlet of which is filled with spawning golden trout. We notice they are thin as smelt. They are not indigenous to these mountains. Around camp, many small trees have been cut by Basque herders whose ubiquitous sheep still graze our wilderness. In autumn we find hunting camps the size of military installations, the hunters better armed than Green Berets. Many of the camps use salt licks to lure the elk, deer, and moose. If we wander out of this narrow "wilderness zone," we walk straight into clear-cut forest, logging roads, and oil wells.

This is not the wild, not a wilderness. And yet we continue to accept it as wilderness and call our time there a wilderness experience. We believe we make contact with the wild, but this is an illusion. In both the national parks and wilderness areas we accept a reduced category of experience, a semblance of the wild nature, a fake. And no one complains.

We visit the zoo or Sea World to see wild animals, but they have been tamed, rendered dependent, obedient. We learn nothing of their essential life in nature. We do not see them hunt or gather food. We do not see them mate. We do not see them interact with other species. We do not see them interact with their habitat. Their numbers and their movements are determined by human artifice. We see them controlled. We see them trained. In most cases they are as docile, apathetic, and bored as the people watching them. If we visit wild animals in sanctuaries, we are protected by buses and Land Rovers and observation towers. We are separated from any direct experience of the wild animals we came to visit.

Even our emotions about the wild are mediated. The majority of people who feel anguish about whales have never seen a whale at sea. The majority of people who want to reintroduce wolves to Yellowstone have never seen a wolf in the wild, and some, no doubt, have never seen Yellowstone. We feel agony about bludgeoned seal pups and shredded dolphins without ever having touched one or smelled one or watched it swim. However much these emotions promote popular environmental causes, they will not preserve wild nature, for the objects of the emotion are usually experienced through movies, TV, the printed word, or snapshots. They are the emotions of an *audience,* the emotions of *sad entertainment,* and they will pass as quickly as our feelings about the evening news or our favorite film.

Dissatisfied with the semblances and imitations at home, we travel abroad in search of the real thing. But there isn't anything different out there, no exotic Other which might afford a perspective on our lives. The context remains, in the apt phrase of George Trow, "the context of no context."[8] We can spend a lifetime in parks and wilderness areas and on adventure-travel trips and remain starved for wild country and wild people.

Thirty years ago no foreigner had set foot in Khumbu, the beautiful valley that approaches Everest from the south. When I started going there twenty years ago, it was advertised as a wilderness, despite the presence of thousands of Sherpas in dozens of villages.

Sometimes it is still advertised that way—an exotic Shangri-la. That this is false is not the point: it is the magnitude of the con that is important, the sheer size of the illusion.

Now, tens of thousands of foreigners visit the region every year. Most arrive by plane at the village of Lukla. The trail from there to the old Everest base camp—"Interstate E"—is always crowded with tourists, many of them in shorts and sandals with Pan Am flight bags over their shoulder containing all they need for several weeks in this "wilderness."

In Namche Bazaar I recently stayed at a hotel owned by a Sherpa I worked with years ago. In the morning I was served the first omelet prepared in the hotel's new microwave oven, the first microwave in Khumbu. It was so hard I barely got it down. The cook, who happens to be the owner's wife, said, "Sherpa way better" and headed back to the kitchen in disgust. Right!

That next winter, electricity came to Thyangboche Monastery and promptly burned it down.

The north side of K2 is more difficult to reach. Fly to Beijing. Fly from Beijing to Urumchi. Fly from Urumchi to Kashgar. Drive two days by Toyota Land Cruiser or Mitsubishi bus to the Chinese army post at Mazar on the long road between Kashgar and Lhasa. Ride camels for a week (they are required for the many fordings of the Shaksgam River). Then walk for several days up a glacier. What do you find? Skeletons of tents, with pieces of nylon flapping in the breeze. Inside are boxes of unused stainless steel pressure cookers, cases of antipasto, and Italian magazines. On a ridge above the glacier is a concrete platform with a radar dish.

Tibet is still described as wild, exotic, and forbidden. At the old British base camp on the north side of Everest is another bare concrete platform, this one awaiting a communications satellite dish that will improve weather predictions for climbing expeditions. Soon there will be a hotel.

When in Lhasa, I stay in a large, modern hotel operated by Holiday Inn. The manager meets me at the door. He is an Englishman, dressed in an impeccable three-piece Saville Row suit, and speaks with an Oxford accent. My room is like any other Holiday Inn room. It has closed-circuit television. In the lobby, during cocktail hour, there is a string quartet that plays Mozart and Beethoven. I drink Guinness stout and Courvoisier cognac. I dine on pasta and yakburgers.

In the streets I see a Red Army soldier driving a lime-green Mercedes Benz. Another soldier drives a cobalt blue Jeep Cherokee. Golok and Khampa nomads wander the bazaar wearing yak-skin boots, woolen breeches, and Tibetan cloaks ("chuba") fringed with snow-leopard fur. They are big men and their hair, entwined with scarlet cloth and gathered on top of their heads, makes them even bigger. One carries a ghetto blaster the size of a small suitcase. The volume makes me wince. He is playing Bruce Springsteen. The preferred style of dress for young male Tibetans in Lhasa is called "Kathmandu Cowboy": black Hong Kong cowboy boots, stone-washed Levi's, a black silk shirt, gold necklace, an Elvis Presley haircut. Young Tibetan women date Chinese soldiers.

I am thankful for the small things. At a monastery outside Lhasa, I saw a senior monk debating with a large gathering of students. He shouted his questions, clapping and stomping to an eight-count beat. His students shouted their answers, trying to keep up with his furious pace, and he continued without slowing. When they failed to answer correctly, he would brush the back of one hand with the back of the other, dismissively smiling and laughing. The students, animated and responsive, would try again.

Once, in the center of Lhasa, I saw a pilgrim circumambulating the Jokhang Monastery through the Barkor Bazaar. He was wearing only yak-skin boots and woolen breeches; in the middle of his back, a gilded prayer box the size of a gallon of milk hung from a thick leather strap slung over one shoulder. He chanted continuously in a strong voice, first holding his hands in prayer high over his head, then bowing hard to the ground—first knees, then chest, then elbows, his hands still held in prayer over his head. Then he would rise, take one step to the left, and repeat his prayer. Though the bazaar was packed with people, there was a forty-foot circle around him. Very few tourists had the temerity to photograph him, and only from a great distance. He is the wildest human being I've seen during twenty years of travel in Asia. A modern Milarepa come from the mountains to honor his gods.

At the Dalai Lama's old summer palace—the Norbulingka—there is a zoo, his private zoo. There are long trenches cut in the ground for yaks and buffalo. All they can see is the sky. There are small cages for wolves and fox and cats and bears. In one cage is a bear the Chinese call "ma-shang." We would call it a grizzly. I think of Buddhism's first great vow: "Beings are numberless: I vow to enlighten them." I try to discover the proper relation between the Dalai Lama, enlightenment, and a caged ma-shang. I feel I have reached the end of a long labyrinth and found a mirror.

These places are beautiful; these people are wonderful. I continue to go there and always will, even knowing full well that I am part of the problem. There are pockets of wilderness left, and a few wild people, but in general, the wilderness and the people of the wilderness are gone. Wild things cannot be reached by travel. We perpetuate the idea that it is out there, we console ourselves with feeble imitations, we seek reassurance in nature entertainment and outdoor sports. But it is nearly gone. Unless we can radically transform modern civilization, the wilderness and its people will be but a memory in the minds of a few people. When they die, it will die with them, and the wild will become completely abstract.

III

What is wrong with all this fun and entertainment, with this imitation of what was once a real and potent Other? Nothing, if it is recognized for what it is—a poor substitute. But we do not note that the wild is missing, and it is not clear how we might reestablish contact with wild things. It is probably best to begin now with what we are emotionally closest to—animals. Plants can come later, places last. Despite all the eco-babble to the contrary, at present we do not have a clue as to what it might mean to communicate with a plant or a place as Native Americans did. Unfortunately, the conditions under which we might form a relationship with wild animals are also diminishing.

The story is repeated daily in the media. A natural habitat is eroded or lost, a species suffers, becomes endangered, or is lost. Efforts are made to save it, study it, and arouse public sympathy for its plight. This always sounds so inevitable, as though the loss of habitat is incorrigible, a matter of fate. There is rarely mention of human agency, an admission that we are responsible for the loss of wilderness habitat, a possibility that we could have done otherwise—that we could reverse this horrible situation, that we have this power—a realization that the abstract language of wildlife management aids and abets the continued loss of wild habitat, an acknowledgment that a zoo, a circus, a Sea World, a national park, is *a business*.

Reading this literature of loss we never discover why an orca like Shamu had to jump through ten thousand hoops to help make millions of dollars for a megacorporation, why she had to abandon her own wild nature so that a handful of humans could make money.

Like torture, training wild animals exhibits the modern complex of truth and power. A real killer whale! It obeys our most trivial wish! Jump, Shamu, jump! Power and truth meet in the body of a live and anguished sentient being. And as with torture, an appreciative audience is required to legitimize the proceedings; what could be the purpose of capturing and training animals if the performance did not amuse the audience?

Zoos are getting bigger and more natural. Wildlife sanctuaries and national parks are islands, too small and increasingly artificial. Yellowstone National Park is really a mega-zoo. *Everything is exploited and managed now; it's just a matter of degree. Accept this. It's normal. We are doing it for the welfare of the animals and their home.*

When we deal in such abstractions, we blur boundaries—between the real and the fake, the wild and the tame, the independent and dependent, the original and the copy, the healthy and the diminished. Blurring takes the edge off loss and removes us from our responsibilities. *Wild nature is not lost; we have collected it; you can go see it whenever you want.*

With the aid of our infinite artifice this fake has replaced the natural. After all, it's not really very different from the original. As Umberto Eco observes in "Travels in Hyperreality," "The ideology of this America wants to establish reassurance through Imitation."[9] And that ideology has succeeded. We are reassured. We are not angry, not even upset, though this abstraction masks horror. Every caricature requires an original—a zoo is a very different *kind* of place from a wild home. A zoo, a Sea World, is (at best) a fake habitat presenting pseudo wild animals to the public for entertainment and financial reward. The wild is the original, the wild is their home. The bigger and more naturalistic the mega-zoo, the better the mask that conceals its reality as a prison for wild animals. Liberal sentiment just demands bigger and nicer cages.

Why we should, or should not, accept the existence of zoos is a subject that cannot be addressed by the abstractions of wildlife science, scientific management, or efficient administration because it questions their legitimacy. From where and from whom does the right come to radio-collar moose, bolt plastic disks to the beaks of ducks, and put polar bears in zoos for a life so boring they must be treated for depression and given unbreakable plastic toys?

The answer to that question is the same for animals as for humans: the state. The state licenses zoos. The state owns all wild animals. Who gave it that power? Did we ever vote on it?

Abstraction displaces emotion, constraining us to relate to wild animals rationally—the excuse of scientific knowledge, commerce, and philanthropy. It leaves us without an explanation of our emotional relations to animals. It cannot explain why I went berserk, amok, at the zoo in Mysore, India, at the sight of a crowd pelting an American mountain lion trapped in a cage on a small wooden platform. This animal was suffering due to a very un-abstract cause. She had probably been sold to a foreign business for amusement and profit, and human beings were mistreating her. Nothing unusual here—normal.

Her suffering was obscene, the solution simple: she needed to get home. To run along rims through pinyon and cedar and crouch and leap and dance on her toes sideways, her tail curled high in the air, to seduce a mate and then hunt with him in the moonlight and eat deer and cows and sheep and make little pumas and die of old age on warm sandstone by a clear spring at the end of a gulch dense with cottonwood and box elder.

The condors need to get home, too. So do the orcas. That they no longer have a home is not their problem. It is our problem; *we* have done it. The solution is to give them their home. Why is this so difficult to conceive or act upon? Part of the answer is this: we no longer have a home except in a brute commercial sense: home is where the bills come. To seriously help homeless humans and animals will require a sense of home that is not commercial. The Eskimo, the Aranda, the Sioux—all belonged to a place. Where is our habitat? Where do I belong?

"All sites of enforced marginalization—ghettos, shanty towns, prisons, madhouses, concentration camps—have something in common with zoos."[10] If we add Indian reservations, aquariums, and botanical gardens to this list, a pattern emerges: removed from their home, living things become marginal, and what becomes marginal is diminished or destroyed. Of bedrock importance is the complexity of animals, plants, and place that creates a unique community. This is as true for *Homo sapiens* as for all other species.

We know that the historical move from community to society

proceeded by destroying unique local structures—religion, economy, food patterns, custom, possessions, families, traditions—and replacing these with national, or international, structures that created the modern "individual" and integrated him into society. Modern man lost his home; in the process everything else did too. That is why Aldo Leopold's land ethic is so frighteningly radical; it renders this process morally wrong: "A thing is right when it tends to preserve the integrity, stability, and beauty of the biotic community. It is wrong when it tends otherwise."[11] Apply this principle to people, animals, and plants, and the last ten thousand years of history is simply evil.

Perhaps the saddest part of this story is the rationale that nature entertainment and recreation *help* the environment. After one orca killed another at Sea World, the veterinarian responsible for the whales tried to justify their captivity, saying that children often "come away with knowledge they didn't have before and a fascination that doesn't go away . . . they become advocates for the marine environment."[12] We hear the same argument about national parks and wilderness areas: they must be entertaining and recreational or the public will not support environmental issues. Contact with exotic cultures is defended by saying it is required to preserve them. In short, the welfare of wild creatures, wild cultures, and wild environments must be useful to modern humans, must fit into our social and economic programs, or they will not be supported.

This argument is no different from the one given by the officer in Vietnam who explained the destruction of a village by saying, "We had to destroy it in order to save it." The first "it" here is real—people, plants, animals, homes—what was destroyed. The second "it" is abstract—a political category—the now nonexistent village we "saved" from the Viet Cong.

What, exactly, is the "it" we are trying to save in all the national parks, wilderness areas, sanctuaries, and zoos? What are we traveling abroad to find? I suggest that, in part, it is something connected with our sense of *home*. If this is even partly true, then we have failed miserably. For intimacy with the fake will not save the real. Many people believe that continued experience with caricatures and simulacra creates a desire to experience the real wild. In my experience, it is more likely to produce a desire for more fakes.

The illusion of contact with the wild provided by national parks, wilderness areas, and Sea Worlds actually diverts us from the wild.

Knowledge gained from these experiences creates an illusion of intimacy that masks our true ignorance and leads to apathy in the face of our true loss. We are inundated by nature, but we do not care about nature.

We might call this failure "Muir's mistake." He did not see clearly enough, if at all, that his experience of the wild—intimate, poetic, and visionary—could never be duplicated by Sierra Club trips and all the other replications of the nature business. In 1895 he told the Sierra Club, "Few are altogether deaf to the preaching of pine-trees. Their sermons on the mountains go to our hearts; and if people in general could be got into the woods, even for once, to hear the trees speak for themselves, all difficulties in the way of forest preservation would vanish."[13]

They got into the woods, but not everyone heard the trees speak. Muir could not have understood that setting aside a wild area would not in itself foster intimacy with the wild. His Yosemite Valley is now more like Coney Island than a wilderness. He could not have known that the organization and commercialization of anything, including wilderness, would destroy the sensuous, mysterious, empathic, absorbed identification he was trying to save and express. He could not have known that even the wild would eventually succumb to consumer culture.

The world of Thoreau and Muir—the mid-nineteenth century—was bright with hope and optimism. In spite of that, they were angry at the loss of the wild and expressed their anger with power and determination. Our times are darker. We understand the difficulties confronting preservation more thoroughly than they did. Their optimism seems impossible at the end of this century. Our world looks backward, obsessed with a dim memory of a world that now seems more—the only word is—real. Something vast and old is vanishing and our rage should mirror that loss.

Refuse to forgive, cherish your anger, remind others. We have no excuses.

It was a place for heathenism and superstitious rites,—to be inhabited by men nearer of kin to the rocks and to wild animals than we. We walked over it with a certain awe, . . . it was a specimen of what God saw fit to make this world. What is it to be admitted to a museum, to see a myriad of particular things, compared with being shown some star's surface, some hard matter in its home! I stand in awe of my body, this matter to which I am bound has become so strange to me. I fear not spirits, ghosts, of which I am one, — *that* my body might, — but I fear bodies, I tremble to meet them. What is this Titan that has possession of me? Talk of mysteries! — Think of our life in nature, — daily to be shown matter, to come in contact with it, — rocks, trees, wind on our cheeks! the *solid* earth! the *actual* world! the *common sense! Contact! Contact!*[14]

3

Mountain Lions

Tiger, Tiger, burning bright
In the forests of the night. . . .
—William Blake

I saw my first mountain lion when I was hunting rabbits at the southeast edge of the Camp Pendleton Marine Corps base in southern California. I was sixteen years old. It was dusk. I was walking through rocky chaparral with a Fox Sterlingworth across my shoulders, my elbows hooked over the stock and barrel and my forearms hanging free—a tired boy not expecting anything special. My mind was on the arroyo ahead. It was sandy and open, scattered with slabs of rock that had spalled off a nearby cliff and were now fringed with thick brush. I decided to walk along the edge and shoot cottontails as they broke into the sandy flats below. Approaching the arroyo, I lowered the gun, slipped the safety, crouched slightly, and walked to the edge.

I saw a tan streak, but I remember, too, the sand flying behind its paws, how low it was to the ground, stretched, and especially the long tail, so long that the tail was its essential feature. Stunned, then elated, I ran after her through the chaparral, but she—for I just knew it a she—was gone.

Not until I was driving home did I realize I'd felt no desire to shoot the lion, an unusual reaction since I shot almost everything then, believing firmly that the world was here for my amusement and that killing was fun. But the lion was different. I have heard wolves howl and seen grizzlies wander high meadows and a tiger feed on a young water buffalo, but no wild animal has captured my imagination like that first lion. I might say she was a totem, but I believe it is simpler than that: I was smitten. I just wanted to see her again, and I often returned to that arroyo with more desire to see her than to hunt.

Years later I teared up over a stuffed female mountain lion at the Bryce Canyon National Park visitor center. This was several decades before it became fashionable for men to weep over dead animals, and I was both angry and embarrassed. Many more years later, in Chicago, I sometimes bought stew meat to surreptitiously feed the mountain lions, snow leopards, and tigers at the zoo. One particularly dark day, deeply depressed by city life, academia, and a failing marriage, I went to the zoo with my stew meat and discovered I no longer knew who felt more caged, the cats or me. And worse, my presence before them confirmed something I no longer wished to confirm. I stopped going to zoos — and slowly began to hate them.

Emotion creates more emotion, and one need not be a Freudian to see that early loves have long, potent causal histories. We come to love before we come to hate, and their loyal metamorphoses and transformations of fear and refuge, rage and consolation, create hard boundaries for the self. I do not believe I would hate zoos if I had not seen that streak, the sand off the paws, the stretch, the long tail. Running through the chaparral with my Fox Sterlingworth that evening long ago, I fell in love.

II

T. E. Lawrence begins *Seven Pillars of Wisdom* with terse words of moral solace: "Some of the evil of my tale may have been inherent in our circumstances" (29). I want to believe this; it somewhat excuses my going amok over a mountain lion at the zoo in Mysore, India.

In the spring of 1981 I was photographing parts of India for Mountain Travel, Inc., a California-based company that organized treks and expeditions to exotic destinations. It was going badly. At the Amber Fort, above Jaipur, I had been chased by a horde of monkeys who screamed in unison and pulled at my pants with their little fingernails. I flew to Bangalore, took the train to Mysore, and met my driver, a Sikh named Singh. (In India, all Sikhs are named Singh, though not all Singhs are Sikhs.) He was a large, genial man with a neat car that reminded me of a Morris. Under the front seat was a pile of rags, and whenever the opportunity arose, Singh dabbed at paint and chrome. Singh drove me to my hotel, where I was meet a former captain in the Gurkhas who still went by that title. That afternoon "Captain" drove me to the old Maharajah of Mysore's hunting lodge by the Kabini River, now part of Nagarhole National Park, where I was to photograph wild elephants.

Proceeding immediately into the jungle, we were directly charged by a bull elephant, ears flapping—the full catastrophe. I got off two shots with the motor drive; the rest were blurs of green as Captain demonstrated remarkable skill at driving backwards down the rutted two-track. This dulled my interest in photographing wild elephants, so we returned to the lodge for a drink— several drinks.

While I was enjoying a cold Star beer, a visiting scientist convinced me we occupied a herpetological paradise of little green vipers, kraits, and cobras, one of which my Navy snake manual described in uncharacteristically poetic prose as "a serpent." He also said there was a healthy population of scorpions, and a "bird-eating" spider as large as his hand that can jump three feet. An employee promptly found one with a dismaying ease and brought it to us in a box. Since I was sleeping in a floorless army tent, I was not amused. Worse, a man had been assigned to spend the whole day—and night—walking around my tent with a stick.

So I was not sleeping well when the monsoon arrived—early, of course. When the tent's lower walls began to cave in from runoff, Captain moved me to the lodge. For my room he chose a narrow dining hall with a long table, high-backed chairs, several elegant cabinets, and a collection of "Bwana pictures"—my name for those early-twentieth-century photographs of immaculately groomed, young European males surrounded by servants and beaters and using dead leopards and tigers as footrests. They invariably held double rifles, something I'd always coveted, so I immediately disliked them. They looked resolute, their faces untroubled by bird-eating spiders, and I have no doubt they died well fighting each other at Verdun.

"Why, exactly, the dining room?" I asked, dumping my pack and duffel on one end of the table. The housekeeper made a squiggly motion with his finger and smiled. I looked at Captain.

"Scorpions," he said. "They live in the furniture and the rains make them active. You had best sleep on the table."

"Really."

I insisted on smiling until they left, then moved the chairs away from the table and rolled out my sleeping bag on the end opposite my pack and duffel. I did not sleep well.

The next morning we retreated to Mysore through mud that occasionally reached the axles of the Land Rover. Singh was waiting for me at the hotel and carried my duffel up to the room. The room had been painted a nauseating peach, it reeked of sandalwood (Mysore's main claim to fame), the bed was canopied, and the linen was a mass of scalloped brocade. Sensing I was at the end of my tether, Singh kindly suggested we go to the zoo so that I might see at least a few of the animals I so obviously could no longer see in the jungle due to the monsoon.

I began fantasizing about hamburgers and chocolate-coated peanut M&Ms. I knew from long experience this meant I needed to get out of Asia. To escape the ghastly room, at least, we went to the Sri Chamarajendra Zoological Garden.

The first animal we saw was a bull elephant whose tusks had been cut off near the base. His right ankle was shackled and a heavy chain bound him to a steel eye set in concrete. ("What the hammer? what the chain? / In what furnace was thy brain?")[1] He would step forward until the chain went slack, then step back for momentum and pull. He did this slowly, with intention. Again and again and again and again and again and again and again. His world had diminished to a simple choice: stand still or execute a small act of resistance.

Numb, spacey with rage, I left the poor beast and went looking for an Asiatic lion, a few of which remain in the Girnar forest in Gujarat. I thought they might be represented in the zoo's collection of cats. I was obviously brain dead and hadn't gotten the elephant's message.

Singh and I ambled on, looking in cages. Singh stopped to read a sign. I kept going, cage by cage. Then a mountain lion was in front of me.

She was small, more gray than tan, with a beautiful cream muzzle and a pink nose. She was immaculately clean. Her small cage contained a wooden loading plaque and a bowl of water — Blake's fearful symmetry, framed by bars.

She showed no affect or attention; she did not move; her eyes stared off to my right. I gazed upon her as if she were kin in slavery, and since, like most men I know, my rage is in direct proportion to my sense of helplessness — and had already been well primed —

I began to sink into that dead-end, rock-bottom, fuck-it pit of rage that is the trademark of my generation.

Perhaps a half dozen young Indian men came up on my left and stood at the rail. The one next to me began to throw a kind of popped grain at the lion. Though several pieces hit her in the face, she still did not move. Perhaps she had been humiliated too much, too often; perhaps she had achieved a state of grace where reaction was beneath her—I do not know. I looked at the man. He smiled at me and threw some more of whatever it was, harder. That was it.

I grabbed his throat and sank my thumb and middle finger into the joint behind his Adam's apple. His eyes went white, he flailed, trying to hit me, but he was too desperate. That's the bitter truth in the fighting acronym NET: nuts, eyes, throat—three vulnerable points where one can lose all semblance of mind. I did not want to kill him, though, not even hurt him. I just wanted to terrify him so badly that he would never, ever, ever, ever again even presume to think of throwing something at that lion.

As I shook him, he grabbed my arms, and we danced away from the cage like a mad couple. Then his friends intervened and we became a clot of bodies. I was big and trained to fight; they were small but many and fought like women, scratching and pulling my ears. Like most fights it was over in seconds. Blood stained the ground, and some of it was mine. Then Singh had his arm around my shoulders and we started for his car, trailing a small angry mob that (forgive me) reminded me of the horde of monkeys at Jaipur. Singh spoke to them in English, Hindi, and a language I did not know. I looked back at the lion. She still had not moved, but now her long tail was in the air and twitching, as when a house cat sees a bird—my only gift to her.

At the car, Singh reached under the driver's seat and handed me his cleaning rags. I dabbed at scratches, a bleeding nose, and a bad eye. At the hotel the concierge was aghast as I dripped blood on his marble floor, and it occurred to me that someone in ancient Rome must have specialized in removing blood from marble. After washing, I went out onto the terrace where Singh was waiting, his eyes still bright with concern. He suggested I leave town. He was willing to drive me. I don't believe I had ever before in my life dismissed someone, but I dismissed Singh. Then I turned and paced the terrace, still on the fine line between that all-too-human rage and its—I must believe this—psychotic expression.

I did not want to leave, I wanted an AK-47. I wanted to go back to the zoo and kill people. I had this absurd thought of leaving the zoo with the lion in my arms. But whom to kill? A fool who throws things at animals? The zoo administrators? (Better.) The son of a bitch who trapped the mountain lion and shipped her to a living death of unending humiliation in a squalid hole in Mysore, India? (Much better.) But that target was not at the zoo, and it is the absence of a responsible target that leads to random violence. Besides, there are approximately 750 accredited zoos in the world, and thousands unaccredited, both public and private. Most of them probably contain mountain lions. So to seriously consider releasing them was tantamount to war.

The heart *does* have it reasons which the reason cannot understand. When I reflect on that day, I produce reasons for my behavior that my culture says do not compute: the lion had no freedom, she was far from home, she was defenseless, she was being humiliated. I construe it now as a matter of dignity; that not doing something would somehow have demeaned me. But at the time I did not "think" at all. Depending on my current theoretical predilections, I explain my behavior to myself as a borderline narcissistic character disorder, an Ugly American syndrome, an ongoing tendency to violence, an identification with wild nature (which for some reason is always assumed to be peaceful), or a particularly bad case of totemic projection—all of which are merely ways of talking around something I don't understand.

I spent quite some time at the end of the terrace, staring down at the bare, rusty red earth into which the rains had carved myriad rivulets. A sudden gestalt switch made them look like southern Utah from 10,000 feet and I wanted to go home and head for the Escalante country.

I turned. Singh was still there.

"You're right," I said, "I should go."

So we drove the rest of that day and on into the night, even though one does not drive at night in India, and slowly we made our way to the famous Jain temple at Sravanabelagola. Before dawn I climbed its granite slabs to meditate. With the first light, Digambara Jains, the world's great pacifists, wandered by, ignoring me. Except for gauze masks over their faces to keep from inhaling insects, they were naked. Shuffling along, they swept their intended paths with long peacock feathers, thus protecting more insects. I wondered what they did about bird-eating spiders and Ugly Americans. I thought their gauze masks and feathers excessive, but I did admire the shelters they maintained for diseased and dying animals. And I longed for their equanimity, for when I tried to meditate, that lion burned in my brain like a torch.

III

In September 1992 I went to dinner in Jackson Hole with my friend Terry Tempest Williams. I often talk with Terry about things I don't usually talk about, or even think about—subjects others might describe as "my feminine side," though I am not inclined to that description.

Terry had just published *Refuge,* a moving remembrance of her mother's death from cancer. My mother had died of cancer the previous year. By the time I reached her side, she was in a coma. Because her kidneys were laced with cancer, because she abhorred doctors and hospitals, and because she was a proud Southern lady appalled by the intrusive medical procedures already performed on her, I declined the offers of surgery and held her hand for four days until she died. Then I buried her ashes with her kin, hard by a forest of redbud and hickory that overlooked the house where she was born. I brought home to Wyoming only a few tokens of our past. One was the family Bible—leather, dating from Revolutionary times, listing our slaves—that they had carried across the Cumberland Gap into eastern Kentucky. Choosing the Bible was perhaps odd, since I had never been a Christian and had always repressed my southern heritage, but then everything was odd. I was still grieving and guilty.

Since my mother's death, the world had become a She. Among the many aspects of this change was a recurring dream of being a teenage girl who had survived an Apocalypse: I rode a tame bull elk named Me; the roads in Jackson Hole were lined with stalled cars filled with decomposed bodies; the Snake River viewed from the Overlook was arrayed with funeral ghats like those at Pashupatinath outside Katmandú; the only humans left were teenage children and three old women, aged versions of three women I loved; when one of them died, all the animals in our valley began to scream; the teenage boys were sterile and did not smell right; I fished the Snake River on a sunny day, bare-breasted and extremely proud of my breasts; I bowed to human bones stuck in the roots of washed-away cottonwood trees, speaking a dream language I called "Kesh" (the language of Ursula Le Guin's *Always Coming Home*), saying an old Pali passage from my Buddhist practice, "Sammasambuddhassa."

I felt *inundated* by the feminine and it was not pleasant. I can talk to Terry about such things without feeling a complete fool, and she will listen and say something insightful and helpful — thus the dinner. So we talked and the evening passed. It was dark when I drove her home.

We drove north on Route 89 to the Gros Ventre Junction, then turned west toward the homes and the golf course south of the Jackson Hole airport.

Suddenly, Terry said, "Moose."

I raised my eyebrows. "See a moose?"

"No, I have just been thinking about moose," she said. "What do you think about when you think about moose?"

"Old, wise, Pleistocene — like bison and pelicans."

"What else?"

"They sometimes sleep on my porch."

"What else?"

"Well, a friend and I once watched a cow moose chase a black bear up a tree three or four times. Just wonderful."

"What else?" Her repetition seemed incantatory now.

The friend I had watched the cow moose and bear comedy with was the old woman in my dream whose death caused the animals to scream and me to have nightmares. She was a student of shamanism.

"She studies shamanism," I said. "I think the moose is one of her power animals, though I don't have the slightest idea what that means."

Casually though, in the back of my mind, I asked myself what my power animal would be if I had a power animal, and my mind replied without hesitation: mountain lion. At that precise moment I noticed an animal running along the other side of the road. It was large and skinny — I thought it was a Great Dane.

Terry said, "It's a mountain lion."

"Give me a break, Terry . . .," but I didn't finish the sentence, because it was, obviously, a mountain lion, loping along the road, and now only a dozen yards in front of us.

I lifted my foot off the gas pedal and we began to coast, catching up with the lion. He was huge, probably a male, unusually bony — you could see his ribs — and he looked old. He seemed unalarmed by our presence. Terry and I had grabbed each other, and that, along with the huskiness of her voice, seemed to sensualize the night. Characteristically, she went straight into her senses and focused on the lion; characteristically, I went straight into my head and started babbling about the lion in Mysore. We stayed like that for awhile, possessed by an island in time. Then the lion crossed the road in front of the car and disappeared into the sagebrush.

Dazzled, we drove to Terry's apartment. She got out, walked to the front of the car, and bowed. I bowed back—and hit my head on the steering wheel.

On the way back to the main highway a woman appeared in my headlights near where we'd seen the lion. She was jogging. I wondered if I should tell her. I lifted my foot from the gas pedal again, but then decided to keep going on the basis of three images in instant succession. The first was a memory of a dead bison sprawled among old mattresses and torn plastic in a nearby rancher's dump. The second was an elderly conservationist I respect saying (about grizzlies), "Don't tell the Park Service where they are, Jack, they're the last people you want to tell." The third was a photograph from *Wildlife Damage Review* that hung above my desk to remind me why I write: eleven mountain lion heads stacked against the base of a cottonwood tree.[2]

Those three images came to mind, and I left the woman to her fate. Then the nasty thought: I will worry about joggers when I see a photograph of eleven joggers' heads stacked under a cottonwood tree. Not very Buddhist of me, to be sure, but there it is. No use lying to enhance the appearance of being a better Buddhist than you are—it's like lying to your diary.

When two more women joggers appeared in the headlights, I felt ludicrously happy, as if their presence had restored my moral stature.

Once home I poured a hit of Herradura from a bottle I keep in the freezer and sat in the rocker on my porch to watch the mountains that rise into the night less than a mile across the meadow. The Park Service translates "the Tetons" as "breasts," though I've been told the French is a bit more slangy. Be that as it may, that night the black breasts looked great against the blue-black sky. Then, as I leaned back in the rocker, I noticed the Milky Way and again the world seemed suffused with a She—a beautiful, necessary, bewitching, claustrophobic She.

For the third time that evening I felt like I'd taken a tad too much Percodan. An aura of prehistory marked the night. Undoubtedly people still have experiences with animals like those of ancient epochs, however unintelligible to our modern lives — unintelligible because we no longer know how to describe them. The vocabularies of shamanism, totems, synchronicities, and She are *tongues again made bold by such experiences,* experiences many believe are irretrievably lost. I believe in the experiences, but I do not understand the vocabularies. I perceive this as my own failing. My life is devoid of practices that might link such events and words. And yet the very existence of such experience is moving — beyond words.

I rocked on my porch in the night and watched my mountains, the walls of my home. The more I thought about the weird evening, the more I appreciated my tequila and the more I cherished my old bony lion. That lion was not a She, and under the circumstances, that was no small consolation.

IV

The autumn of 1992 was dry in the Tetons. Since little snow had fallen, the Park Service kept the road open through Grand Teton National Park, and though there was eight to ten inches of snow on the ground, people continued to drive into the park. Early on November 21, I drove up from Moose to my cabin and set off to walk the seven miles around Jenny Lake. The temperature was 2°F and an icy fog hung low, the cottonwoods and willows rimed by mist coming off Cottonwood Creek.

From the cabin I crossed a quarter mile of meadow to reach the lake trail. Using ski poles for balance, I walked on what was in summer a dirt road to the little parking lot just west of the meadow. From there, I struck north on a path to the main trail and wandered around the lake, painting watercolors and writing in my journals. When the fog cleared, the day became cloudless, crystalline, calm, and cold.

When I recrossed my trail by the bridge over Cottonwood Creek that evening, I saw large cat tracks with tail-drag marks in the snow. The edges were crusty from the afternoon melt. It was my lion. A Yellowstone ranger climbing Guide's Wall had seen him in Cascade Canyon, and he had been sighted twice by tourists at the Windy Point turnout.

I walked to the cabin, got a tape measure, a head lamp, and my old green copy of Murie's *A Field Guide to Animal Tracks*. The paw prints varied from three and a quarter to four inches, but I realized that the lion stepping in his own tracks and also, no doubt, the melting had enlarged them. The straddle measurement was thirteen inches, and the stride varied from twenty to twenty-eight inches, with one jump of thirty-eight inches. From the prints and tail-drag marks, I figured the lion was eight feet long from his nose to the tip of his tail.

After wandering about by the bridge, the lion had followed me across the meadow as far as I could see, walking directly over my right ski pole marks. He was intent: the prints were so consistent they could have been made by a machine. I did not like the fact this was the second time I had found him on a road, and I did not like the fact he had tracked me, most likely in the early morning fog. I did not like the fading light. I remembered his ribs. He was probably on his last leg and having difficulty hunting.

I followed our tracks across the meadow, and as I left the little parking lot and the path narrowed, the tracks moved left, over my footprints. I was wearing Vibram soles and the section under the ball of the foot was about four inches wide—I noticed the similarity of size. Then his prints split a bit more, no longer in direct registration, as they say, but slightly behind one another and slightly off center, so the combined print of the front and hind paws merged and grew larger.

Then one paw stepped directly into my boot track, mostly erasing it—like one signature canceling another. Just my toe stuck out in front of his print, like something hanging out of a mouth. I stopped, my foot in mid-air, and felt the cold stab of terror in the stomach that means something is badly wrong. I carefully stepped backwards and looked around. The sky behind Teewinot was the palest blue and pink of opals. The sun was down, the wind was dispatching plumes of snow from the summit six thousand feet above. To the east the sky was menacing, the gun-barrel blue of the Earth's shadow supporting banks of carmine clouds. In my paranoid imagination the colors reminded me of a bad wound. There was no sound but the wind in the forest. For perhaps a minute I was paralyzed, my will absorbed by a presence.

Until then I had no fear of mountain lions. I knew that, statistically, I had little to worry about. During the hundred years from 1890 until 1990 there were only fifty-three recorded attacks on humans by mountain lions in both the United States and Canada, only ten people died, and 64 percent of the deaths were children. Human beings killed more than a hundred million other human beings during the same period and we weren't even hungry, so it seems reasonable to make room for lions.

But terror is not a matter of statistics. Confronted with Blake's forest of the night, I faltered. I had no sense of this lion, or any lion; no expectation of what he might do, no knowledge, no tradition to help me know how to act. Traditions bring the unknown into the circle of our lives and give it form and a practice that manages its Otherness. Those who love wild predators lack such a tradition, thus our discontent. As Wittgenstein says somewhere, a man without a tradition, who wants one, is like a man unhappily in love. When I observe the great curiosity that wild animals sometimes have for me, I wonder if they feel a similar discontent. Or are we always Other to them, *their terror?*

We do not lack information about *Felis concolor*. The literature, both general and technical, is vast, and Harley Shaw's *Soul Among Lions* is a masterpiece of natural history. But information does not a tradition make, and virtually all of it is determined by two activities: hunting and science. I am not interested in these ways of relating to mountain lions, so for me this vast literature is mostly worthless. Instead I am interested in a possible future tradition. I want to know how our relationship to wild predators might become, let me say, friendly and respectful — a peaceful covenant.

Since this strikes most people as absurd, an example is in order. "The Old Way," Elizabeth Marshall Thomas's remarkable essay on the Juwa Bushmen and the African lion, describes just such a peaceful covenant between humans and a large predator. It should be studied by anyone who loves the wild.

Until the past few decades, the Bushmen and the lions lived among each other. They shared water holes. Prides occasionally came into Bushmen camps. A small group of four Bushmen hunters could drive a pride of thirty lions off a wildebeest killed by a Bushman. A lone and unarmed Bushman would often encounter a lion while out gathering, and both lion and human could handle the situation by what can only be called an etiquette.

The Juwa Bushmen could not defend themselves against a lion. Their spears, unlike the spears of the Masai, were too short. They carried no shields. Their bows were too delicate. They hunted primarily with poison arrows that took so long to kill, they offered no immediate protection, though they would, over time, kill a lion.

Although Bushmen could kill lions, they choose not to; and although lions could kill Bushmen, they choose not to. A genealogical study conducted by Thomas's brother, John Marshall, and Claire Ritchie, involving more than three thousand Bushmen and going back nearly a hundred years, found only one instance of a lion killing a Bushman, and this was a young paraplegic girl. And Thomas knew of no lion killed by the Juwa.

These salient facts surely merit considerable thought and suggest future possibilities for our own relations with mountain lions, grizzlies, and wolves. Contrary to popular belief, most (not all) American Indians failed spectacularly to establish peaceful covenants with predators. We cannot expect to have a friendly, respectful relationship with predators we hunt — for whatever reason. North Americans have only rarely lived a decent covenant with predators, and our current inability to go beyond historical forms of failure simply confirms the poverty of our imagination. No one has the slightest idea what to do about it.

The old lion and I shared no covenant, thus my unreasonable terror. With a mixture of sadness and fear, I turned tail and headed back across the meadow, nursing a severe case of over-the-shoulder-itis.

Late that night it snowed. The next morning I went back to Jenny Lake and searched for tracks. A herd of elk grazed some high grasses on the lower slopes of Teewinot. The snowshoe rabbits were active along the creek. There was an unusual number of weasels about, and a few mule deer near the Moose Ponds. But no mountain lion.

That night it snowed again. The road into the park was closed. I skied out to the lake along the road — still a bit spooked by the forests, even during the day — as bad a symptom for this old mountaineer as walking paved roads was for an old mountain lion. The elk had moved off Teewinot onto the sagebrush flats east of Timbered Island. The deer tracks showed they had gone down Cottonwood Creek, heading toward their winter range on the Gros Ventre Buttes. I carefully searched the new snow with my glasses and spotting scope but found no cat tracks. Winter was upon us and the old lion was gone.

4

Economic Nature

The conservation movement is, at the very least,
an assertion that these interactions between man and land are
too important to be left to chance, even that sacred variety
of chance known as economic law. — Aldo Leopold

We live surrounded by scars and loss. Each of us carries around
a list of particular offenses against our place: a clear-cut, an over-
grazed meadow, a road, a dam. Some we grudgingly accept as
necessary, others we judge mistakes. The mistakes haunt us like
demons, the demons spawn avenging spirits, and the presence of
demons and spirits helps make a place our home. It is not accidental that "home" and "haunt" share deep roots in Old English, that
we speak of the home of an animal as its haunt, or that "haunt"
can mean both a place of regular habitation and a place marked
by the presence of spirits. Like scars, the spirits are reminders —
traces by which the past remains present.

Forty years ago big cutthroats cruised the Gros Ventre River of
Jackson Hole, Wyoming. Now, in late summer, dust blows up the
river bed. It's as dry as an arroyo in Death Valley, a dead river
drained by ranchers. Each autumn much of Jackson Lake, the jewel
of Grand Teton National Park, is a mud flat baking in the sun,
its waters drained to irrigate potatoes. Without good snowfalls
each winter the lake could disappear and with it the big browns,
and with those browns, Gerard Manley Hopkins' "rose moles all
in stipple upon trout that swim."[1] The western border of Yellowstone National Park can be seen from outer space, a straight line
cut through a once fine forest by decades of clearcutting. From the
summits of the Tetons, I see to the west a mosaic of farms scar-
ring the rounded hills and valleys, as though someone had taken
a razor to the face of a beautiful woman. Farther west, the sock-

eye salmon no longer come home from the sea. The rivers are wounded by their absence.

These wounds and scars are not random. We attribute the damage to particular people or corporations or to generalities like industrialization, technology, and Christianity, but we tend to ignore the specific unity that made *these* particular wounds possible. This unity lies in the resource economies of the West: forestry, grazing, mineral extraction, and the vast hydrological systems that support agriculture. Healing those wounds requires altering these economies, their theories, practices, and most deeply and importantly, their descriptions of the world, for at the most fundamental level the West has been wounded by particular uses of language.

Modern economics began in postfeudal Europe with the social forces and intellectual traditions we call the Enlightenment. On one level, its roots are a collection of texts. Men in England, France, and Germany wrote books; our Founders read the books and in turn wrote letters, memoranda, legislation, and the Constitution, thus creating a modern civil order of public and private sectors. Most of the problems facing my home today stem from that duality: water rights, the private use of public resources, public access through private lands, the reintroduction of wolves into Yellowstone National Park, wilderness legislation, the private cost of grazing permits on public lands, military overflights, nuclear testing, the disposal of toxic waste, county zoning ordinances — the list is long. We are so absorbed by these tensions, and the means to resolve them, that we fail to notice that our maladies share a common thread — the use of the world conceived of as a collection of resources.

Almost everyone agrees the use of public and private resources is out of kilter, but here agreement ends. This absence of agreement is the key to our difficulties, not, for instance, the cost of grazing fees.

A civil society is marked by a barely conscious consensus of beliefs, values, and ideals — of what constitutes legitimate authority, on what symbols are important, on what problems need resolution, and on limits to the permissible. I think of this consensus as a shared vision of the good. Historically, our shared vision of the good derived from shared experience and interests in a shared place. In the West, these "sharings" have vanished — assuming, of course, they ever existed. We share no vision of the good, especially concerning economic practices. One of many reasons for this is the growing realization that our current economic practices are creating an unlivable planet.

The decline in consensus also erodes trust. Trust is like glue — it holds things together. When trust erodes, personal relations, the family, communities, and nations delaminate. To live with this erosion is to experience modernity.[2] The modern heirs of the Enlightenment believe material progress is worth the loss of shared experience, place, community, and trust. Others are less sanguine. But in the absence of alternatives the feeling of dilemma becomes paramount: most of us in the West feel stuck.

Daniel Kemmis's fine book *Community and the Politics of Place* traces some of the West's current dilemmas to the often conflicting visions of Jefferson and Madison, and no doubt some of our dilemmas can be discussed productively in this context. But I think the problems lie deeper. After all, Jefferson and Madison derived their ideas from the works of Enlightenment figures, especially John Locke and Adam Smith, men whose thought was a mixture of classical science, instrumental reason, and Christian revelation.

The heirs of Locke and Smith are the members of the so-called Wise Use movement. Its vigor derives from an accurate assessment: the social order they believe in *requires* Christian revelation, pre-Darwinian science, pre-particle physics, and a model of reason as the maximization of utility. The accuracy of this assessment, in turn, disturbs both liberals and conservatives who wish to preserve Enlightenment ideals while jettisoning the Christian foundations upon which those ideals rest. Unfortunately, that reduces social theory to economics. As John Dunn concluded twenty-five years ago in *The Political Thought of John Locke,* " 'Lockean' liberals of the contemporary United States are more intimately than they realize the heirs of the egalitarian promise of Calvinism. If the religious purpose and sanction of the calling were to be removed from Locke's theory, the purpose of individual human life and of social life would both be exhaustively defined by the goal of the maximization of utility" (250). That's where we are now. Instead of a shared vision of the good, we have a collection of property rights and utility calculations.

Since I am a Buddhist, I do not restrict equality to human beings, nor do I justify it by Christian revelation. Nor do I see any reason to restrict "common" (as in "the common good") or "community" to groups of human beings. Other citizens of the West have different understandings and justifications of these key political terms, so part of the solution to the West's differences involves language.

Between Newton and the present, the language of physical theory changed and our conception of reality has changed with it. Unfortunately, the languages of our social, political, and economic theories have endured despite achieving mature formulation before widespread industrialization, the rise of technology, severe overpopulation, the explosion of scientific knowledge, and globalization of economies. These events altered our social life without altering theories *about* our social life. Since a theory is merely a description of the world, a new set of agreements about the West requires some new descriptions of the world and our proper place in it.

Against this background, environmentalism, in the broadest sense, is a new description of the world. The first imaginings of the movement have led to what *Newsweek* has called "the war for the West." Attorney Karen Budd, who often supports Wise Use agendas, says, "The war is about philosophy," and she's right.[3] The fight is over intellectual, not physical, resources. Environmentalists fight to reduce the authority of certain descriptions—e.g., "private property"—and to extend the authority of other descriptions—e.g., "ecosystem." It is the language of pilgrims who entered the wilderness and found not Him, but the Wild.

These new forces have occupied the border of our minds—strange figures claiming high moral ground, like Sioux along the ridges of the Missouri. It's unsettling. Folks employed in traditional economies are circling the wagons of old values and beliefs. Their tone and posture is defensive, as it must be for those who, hurled into the future, adamantly cling to the past.

II

The pioneers who settled the West imposed their descriptions on a place they called wilderness and on people they called savages. Neither were, by definition, a source of moral value. The great debates of Jefferson, Madison, Hamilton, and Adams were filled with Enlightenment ethics, revelation, science, political theory, and economic theory. The pioneers brought these ideas west to create a moral and rational order in a new land. Their ideas of what was moral and rational were connected by economics.

The government's great surveys redescribed the western landscape. In 1784 the federal government adopted a system of rectangular surveying first used by the French for their national survey. The result was a mathematical grid: six-mile squares, one-mile squares.[4] Unfold your topo map and there they are, little squares everywhere. Fly over a town or city and you will see people living in a matrix resembling a computer chip. The grid also produced rectangular farms, national parks, counties, Indian reservations, and states, none of which have any relation to the biological order of life.

The grid delighted the pioneers though; they believed a rationalized landscape was a good landscape. It was a physical expression of order and control — the aim of their morality. The idea, of course, was to sell the grid for cash. Indeed, the selling of the grid was the primary reason for its existence. This shifted the locus of the sacred from place to private property. As John Adams said, "Property must be sacred or liberty cannot exist." So the grid was sold to farmers, ranchers, and businessmen, and the places long sacred to the indigenous population simply vanished behind the grid, behind lines arrogantly drawn on paper. With the places gone, the sense of place vanished too — just disappeared.

The sale didn't work out quite as planned. Some land was sold, but often for as little as $1.25 an acre. Other land passed "free" to those who worked it. What was not sold became public land or was reserved to imprison the remnants of the indigenous population. Much of it was simply given to commercial interests.

The railroads alone received 233 million acres. For comparison, consider that Yellowstone National Park's boundaries encompass 2.3 million acres, and that in 1993 our entire national park system — including parks, national monuments, historic sites, historic parks, memorials, military parks, battlefields, cemeteries, recreational areas, lake shores, seashores, parkways, scenic trails, and rivers, in the lower forty-eight *and* Alaska — totals 79 million acres. Consider also that 59 percent of our wilderness areas (which, combined, total 91 million acres) are smaller than Disney World.

Agricultural practices forever destroyed the autonomy of the land sold to farmers and ranchers. Jefferson wrote that "those who labor in the earth are the chosen people of God, if ever He had a chosen people, whose breasts He has made His peculiar deposit for substantial and genuine virtue. It is the focus in which he keeps alive that sacred fire, which otherwise might escape from the face of the earth."[5] God's chosen perceive it good to move water around with irrigation systems; they perceive it good to introduce foreign species of plants and animals; they perceive it good to destroy all that is injurious to their flocks and gardens. In short, they perceive as good that which is good for farmers and ranchers.

Federalists were less convinced of the inherent goodness of farmers, and in retrospect, of course, they were correct. (After all, farmers had burned women at the stake in New England, and, in other parts of the world still boiled and ate their enemies.) Their solution was a federal system of checks and balances. Just as the free market would transform the pursuit of economic self-interest into the common good, so a federal government would transform the pursuit of political self-interest into the common good. Unfortunately, the pursuit of self-interest merely produced more self-interest, an endless spiral that we now recognize as simple greed.

In short, the social order of the American West was a mishmash of splendid ideals and pervasive blindness — a rationalized landscape settled by Christians holding private property as sacred and practicing agriculture and commerce under the paternal eye of the federal government. Eventually, of course, these forces proved unequal in power and effect.

Things change. Governmental regulations, commercial greed, and the expanding urban population gobbled up family farms, ranches, and communities, and left in their place industrial agriculture, large tracts of empty land held by banks, subdivisions, and malls. In Wyoming, for instance, only 2 percent to 4 percent of jobs now depend on agriculture.

Things change. The little squares got smaller and smaller as the scale of the social order changed. First there was the section, then the acre, then the hundred-foot lot, then wall-to-wall town houses, then condos. Last year the town of Jackson, Wyoming, contemplated building three-hundred-square-foot housing — about the size of a zoo cage. Most people live in tiny rented squares and the ownership of sacred property is an aging dream. The moral force of private property, derived from owning land, usually large amounts of land, has dropped accordingly. For most people, the problems connected with large holdings of private land are inconsequential. Asking citizens to lament the government's incursion into private-property rights increasingly obliges them to feel sorry for the rich, an obligation that insults their sense of justice.

Things change. The federal system of checks and balances consistently stalls and sabotages federal legislation, making hash of federalism. Every time Congress meets, it is pressured to gut the Clean Air Act and the EPA. Despite widespread regional and national support, twenty years elapsed between the passage of the Endangered Species Act and the reintroduction of wolves in Yellowstone.

Things change. Even the mathematical grid is under attack. The idea that our social units should be defined by mathematical squares projected upon Earth from arbitrary points in space appears increasingly silly. One result is the interest in bioregionalism, the view that drainage, flora, fauna, land forms, and the spirit of a place should influence culture and social structure, define its boundaries, and ensure that evolutionary processes and biological diversity persist.

Things change. A new generation of historians have redescribed our past, deflating the West's myths with rigorous analysis of our imperialism, genocide, exploitation, and abuse; our vast hierarchies of wealth and poverty; the collusion of the rich and the government, especially over water; the biological and ecological ignorance of many farmers, ranchers, and capitalists; and, finally, how our old histories veiled the whole mess with nods to Republican and Jeffersonian ideals. Anyone who bothers to read the works of Donald Worster, Dee Brown, Patricia Nelson Limerick, and Richard White will be stripped forever of the comfortable myths of pioneer and cowboy.[6]

Few, I believe, would deny these changes, and yet in our public discourse of hearings and meetings and newspaper editorials we continue to trade in ideas appropriate to a small homogeneous population of Christian agriculturists occupying large units of land. We continue to believe that politicians represent people, that private property assures liberty, and that agriculture, commerce, and federal balances confer dignity and respect on the West and its people. Since this is largely illusion, it is not surprising that we face problems.

Only one widely shared value remains — money — and this explains our propensity to use business and economics rather than moral debate and legislation to settle our differences. When "the world" shrinks into a rationalized grid stuffed with resources, greed goes pandemic.

Many conservation and preservation groups now disdain moral persuasion, and many have simply given up on government regulation. Instead, they purchase what they can afford or argue that the market should be used to preserve everything from the ozone layer to biodiversity. They offer rewards to ranchers who allow wolves to den on their property, they buy trout streams, they pay blackmail so the rich will not violate undeveloped lands. They defend endangered species and rain forests on economic grounds. Instead of seeing modern economics as the problem, they see it as the solution.

This rejection of persuasion creates a social order wherein economic language (and its extensions in law) exhaustively describes our world and, hence, *becomes* our world. Moral, aesthetic, cultural, and spiritual orders are then merely subjective tastes of no social importance. It is thus no wonder that civility has declined. For me this new economic conservation "ethic" reeks of cynicism — as though having failed to persuade and woo your love, you suddenly switched to cash. The new economic conservationists think they are being rational; I think they treat Mother Nature like a whorehouse.

Ironically, the Enlightenment and civil society were designed to rescue us from such moral vacuums. The Enlightenment taught that human beings need not bow to a force beyond themselves, neither church nor king. Now we are asked to bow to markets and incentives.

Shall we bow to the new king? Can the moral concerns of the West be resolved by economics? Can new incentives for recycling, waste disposal, and more efficient resource use end the environmental crisis? Can market mechanisms restore the quality of public lands? Does victory lie in pollution permits, tax incentives, and new mufflers? Will green capitalism preserve biodiversity? Will money heal the wounds of the West?

One group that answers these questions in the affirmative is New Resource Economics. It welcomes the moral vacuum and fills it with markets and incentives. As economic theory it deserves scrutiny by economists. I am not an economist but a mountaineer and desert rat. Nonetheless, I shall have my say even though the word "economics" makes me hiss like Golem in Tolkien's *The Hobbit:* "I hates it, I hates it, I hates it *forever.*" For I believe classical economic theory, and all the theories it presupposes, is destroying the magic ring of life.

III

In the winter of 1992 I flew to Seattle at the generous invitation of the Foundation for Research on Economics and the Environment to attend a conference designed to acquaint environmental writers with the ideas of New Resource Economics. The conference was held amidst a mise-en-scène of assurance and power — tasteful, isolated accommodations, lovely meals, good wine. I felt like a barbarian called to Rome to applaud its splendor.

The best presentations were careful, devastating analyses of the inefficiency and incompetence of the U.S. Forest Service. In sharp contrast were other presentations with vague waves at the preferred vocabulary of self-interest: incentives, market, liberty. They exuded an attitude of *"You see!"* as though the realm of sylvan possibilities was limited to two choices: socialism or New Resource Economics. They were Eric Hoffer's true believers, folks who had seen the light and are frustrated and angry that others fail to see economics as the solution to our environmental plight.

I not only failed to see the light, I failed to understand what was new about New Resource Economics. The theory applies ideas about markets that are now more than two hundred years old. After awhile I had the feeling of watching the morally challenged tinker with notions rapidly disappearing over the horizon of history as they attempted to upgrade one antiquated idea into another. And yet I have little doubt they will succeed.

Having just flown over the devastated forests east of Seattle, I wanted to scream, "See the fate of the Earth, the rape of the land!" — but I knew they would respond calmly with talk of incentives and benefits and inefficiency.

Finally I understood. The conference's hidden agenda was to persuade environmental writers to describe nature with an economic vocabulary. They had a theory, and like everyone with a theory, they were attempting to colonize with their theoretical vocabulary, thus eliminating other ways of describing the world.

The conference literature reeked of colonization. Vernon L. Smith's paper, *Economic Principles in the Emergence of Humankind,* describes magic, ritual, and foraging patterns in hunter-gatherer cultures with terms like "opportunity cost," "effort prices," and "accumulated human capital."[7] Michael Rothchild, in *Bionomics: Economy as Ecosystem,* extends economic vocabulary to ecosystems and animal behavior; a niche becomes an organism's "profession," its habitat and food "basic resources," its relations to habitat simply a part of the "economy of nature."

In *Reforming the Forest Service*, Randal O'Toole claims that "although the language used by ecologists differs from that of economists, it frequently translates into identical concepts. Where economists discuss efficiency, decentralization, and incentives, ecologists discuss the maximum power principle, diversity, and feedback loops." O'Toole also maintains that "these very different terms have identical meanings," and he concludes that "ecological systems are really economic systems, and economic systems are really ecological systems" (193).

The redescription of everything with economic language is characteristic of those who sit in the shade of the Chicago school of economics. Thus Richard Posner, in *The Economic Aspects of Law*, colonizes legal issues with economic vocabulary. Regarding children, Posner thinks "the baby shortage and black market are the result of legal restrictions that prevent the market from operating as freely in the sale of babies as of other goods. This suggests as a possible reform simply eliminating the restriction."[8] Bunker, Barnes, and Mosteller's *Costs, Risks, and Benefits of Surgery* does the same for medical treatment.

Indeed, all areas of our social life have been redescribed in economic language. If you like the theory in one area, you will probably like it everywhere. Nor is economic redescription limited to social issues. For example, Robert Nozick, in *The Examined Life*, applies economic language to the question of why we might love our spouse.

> Repeated trading with a fixed partner with special resources might make it rational to develop in yourself specialized assets for trading with that partner (and similarly on the partner's part toward you); and this specialization gives some assurance that you will continue to trade *with that party* (since the invested resources would be worth much less in exchanges with any third party). Moreover, to shape yourself and specialize so as to better fit and trade with that partner, and therefore to do so less well with others, you will want some commitment and guarantee that the party will continue to trade with you, a guarantee that goes beyond the party's own specialization to fit you. (77–78)

In a footnote, Nozick says, "This paragraph was suggested by the mode of economic analysis found in Oliver Williamson, *The Economic Institutions of Capitalism.*"

Why stop with love? In *The New World of Economics* by McKenzie and Tullock, sex becomes a calculated rational exchange.

> [I]t follows that the quantity of sex demanded is an inverse function of price. . . . The reason for this relationship is simply that the rational individual will consume sex up to the point that the marginal benefits equal the marginal costs. . . . If the price of sex rises relative to other goods, the consumer will "rationally" choose to consume more of the other goods and less sex. (Ice cream, as well as many other goods, can substitute for sex if the relative price requires it.)[9]

So, many men are bores, and what to do? Why bother with arguments, why not just giggle? Unfortunately, too much is at stake.

If we are to preserve a semblance of democracy in the West, we must become crystal clear about how economists colonize with their language.

To start, look at an example of redescription by a theory I disapprove of. Consider, for instance, psycho-babble.

"What did you do today?"

"I cleaned my desk."

"Ah yes, being *anal compulsive* again."

"No, it was just a mess."

"No need to be *defensive.*"

"I'm not being *defensive,* I'm just disagreeing with you."

"Yes, but you disagree with me because you have an *unresolved conflict* with your father."

"No, I always got along well with Dad."

"Of course you believe that, but the conflict was *unconscious.*"

"There was no conflict!"

"I am not your father! Please don't *cathect* your speech with *projected aggression.*"

Ad infinitum. Ad nauseam.

Resource, market, benefits, rational, property, self-interest function the same way as *conflict, unconscious, cathect,* and *projected aggression.* They are simply the terms a particular theory uses to describe the world. By accepting those descriptions, you support and extend the theory. You could decide to ignore the theory, or conclude that the theory is fine in its limited context but shouldn't be extended into others. But if we don't want the fate of our forests decided by bar graphs, we need to cease talking about forests as measurable resources. That does not require you to stop talking to your investment banker about the bar graphs in her analysis of your portfolio.

Economists and scientists have conned us into speaking of trees as "resources," wilderness as a "management unit," and picas gathering grass for the winter because of "incentives." In accepting their descriptions, we allow a set of experts to define our concerns in economic terms and predetermine the range of possible responses. Often we cannot even raise the issues important to us because the economic language of others excludes our issues from the discussion. To accept this con emasculates not only radical alternatives, but all alternatives. Every vocabulary shapes the world to fit a paradigm. If you don't want nature reduced to economics, then *refuse to use its language.*

This process of theoretical redescription has been termed "colonization" because it privileges one description of the world and excludes others. The Sioux say the Black Hills are "sacred land," but they have found that "sacred land" does not appear in the language of property law. There is no office in which to file a claim for sacred land. If they filed suit, they'd discover that the Supreme Court tends to protect religious belief but not religious practices in a particular place—a very Protestant view of religion.

Language is power. Control people's language and you won't need an army to win the war for the West. There will be nothing to debate. If we are conned into describing the life of the Earth and our home in terms of benefits, resources, self-interest, models, and budgets, then democracy will be dead.

What to do? I have five suggestions.

First, refuse to talk that way. It's like smoking, or eating lard. Just say no, and point out that your concerns cannot be expressed in that language.

Second, develop a talent for light-hearted humor using economic language. Here again, Thoreau was a prophet. Henry knew a great deal about economics. He read Locke and his followers in both his junior and senior years at Harvard; he was acquainted with the ideas of Smith, Ricardo, Say, and Franklin; and he helped run his family's pencil business when the industry was becoming increasingly competitive and undergoing rapid change. But Thoreau flips economic language on its head. (Remember, the first chapter of *Walden* is titled "Economy.") His "trade" turns out to be with the Celestial Empire; his "enterprises" are inspecting snow storms and sunrises; he "sinks his capital" into hearing the wind; he "keeps his accounts" by writing in his journal; and he gleefully carries the cost of rye meal out to four decimal places: $1.0475. Nothing is fixed, all is metaphor, even economics.

Third, become so intimate with the process of economic description, you *experience* what's wrong with it. Since economics is a world of resources—physical resources, cultural resources, recreational resources, visual resources, human resources—our wonderfully diverse, joyful world must be reduced to measurable resources. This involves abstraction, translation, and a value. Just as time is abstracted from experience and rendered mechanical (the clock) so it can be measured, space is abstracted from place and becomes property: measurable land. In the same way, trees are abstracted into board-feet, wild rivers are abstracted into acre-feet, and beauty is abstracted into a scene whose value is measured by polls.

Economics reduces everything to a unit of measurement because it requires that everything be commensurate—"capable of being measured by a common standard"—its standard. The variety of these calculable units may be great—board-feet, time, tons, hours—but all of these units can be translated into a common value similar to the way different languages can be translated. Both types of translation require something common. In linguistic translation, it is meaning; in economic translations, it is money—not the change in your pocket, but the stuff that blips on computer screens and bounces off satellite dishes from Germany to Japan in less than a second. An hour's labor is worth a certain amount of money; so is three hundred board-feet of redwood.

Once everything is abstracted into commensurate units and common value, economic theory is useful. If the value of one kind of unit (computer chips) grows in value faster than another kind of unit (board-feet), economic theory says translate board-feet into money into computer chips. In ordinary English: Clear-cut the last redwoods for cash and buy Intel stock. If you don't like deciding the fate of redwoods by weighing the future of Intel, then you probably won't like economics.

Refuse these three moves—the abstraction of things into resources, their commensurability in translatable units, and the choice of money as the value of the units—and economic theory is useless.

Once you understand the process, it's easy to recognize examples. For instance, in *Reforming the Forest Service*, Randal O'Toole describes walking in the mountains as a wilderness experience using a recreational resource that generates benefits: cash and jobs (206). These benefits are compared to other possible uses of the resource, say, grazing and logging, that generate other benefits. The benefits can then be compared. This provides a rational basis for budget maximization. Your walk in the Tetons becomes, by redescription, an economic event.

A fourth way to subvert economic language is to realize that nothing of great value is either abstract or commensurate. Start with your hand. The workman's compensation office can tell you the value of your hand in dollars. Consider your daughter. An insurance company or litigation lawyer can tell you her value in dollars. What is your home place worth? Your lover's hair? A stream? A species? Wolves in Yellowstone? Carefully imagine each beloved person, place, animal, or thing redescribed in economic language. Then apply cost-benefit analysis. What results is a feeling of sickness familiar from any forest sale or predator-control proposal. It is the sickness of being forced to use a language that ignores what matters in your heart.

Finally, realize that describing life—the completely individual, unique here-now alive *this*—with abstractions is especially dissonant. Consider the "resources" used in a biology class. The founder of experimental physiology, Claude Bernard, said that the man of science "no longer hears the cry of animals, he no longer sees the blood that flows, he sees only his idea and perceives only organisms concealing problems which he intends to solve."[10] He sees only the idea that will give him something to do in the world. Meanwhile the screams of animals in laboratory experiments are redescribed as "high-pitched vocalizations."

In an extraordinary essay, "Pictures at a Scientific Exhibition," William Jordon, an entomologist, describes his graduate education and the ghastly (his word) treatment of animals it required.

Fifteen years ago I saw several of my peers close down their laboratory for the evening, and as they cleaned up after the day's experimentation they found that three or four mice were left over. The next experiments were not scheduled for several weeks, and *it wasn't worth the cost and effort to keep the mice alive until then.* My friends simply threw the extras into a blender, ground them up, and washed them down the sink. This was called the Bloody Mary solution. Several days ago I talked with another old peer from my university days, and she informs me that the new, humane method for discarding extra mice in her lab is to seal them in a plastic bag and put it in the freezer.

I repeat: the attitude toward nonhuman life has not changed among experimental biologists. Attitude is merely a projection of one's values, and their values have not changed; they do not respect life that is not human. (199, my emphasis)

Science, including economics, tends to reduce nonhuman life to trash. The screaming animals, the dead coyotes, the Bloody Mary mice, the stumps, the dead rivers—all are connected by these processes of abstraction, commensurability, and financial value. There is no logical necessity for us to describe the world this way. The Apaches didn't do it, and we need to reach a point where we don't do it either.

We need to find another way of describing the world and our experience in it. Leave this pernicious, mean-spirited way of talking behind. One of my heroes said he could imagine no finer life than to arise each morning and walk all day toward an unknown goal forever. Basho said this *is* our life. So go for a walk and clear the mind of this junk. Climb right up a ridge, over the talus and through the whitebark pine, through all those charming little grouse wortleberries, and right on into the blue sky of Gary Snyder's *Mountains and Rivers Without End:*

> the blue sky
> the blue sky
>
> The Blue Sky
> is the land of
> OLD MAN MEDICINE BUDDHA
> where the eagle
> that flies out of sight,
>
> flies.[11]

Traveling to that conference last winter, I found the approach to Seattle from the east to be infinitely sad. Looking down at those once beautiful mountains and forests, so shaved and mowed down they look like sores, I didn't care if the land below was public or private, if the desecration was efficient or inefficient, cost beneficial, or subsidized, whether the lumber products were sent to Japan or used to build homes in Seattle. I was no longer interested in that way of looking at the world. Increasingly, I am a barbarian in the original sense of the Greek word — one who has trouble with the language of civilization. So, slowly and reluctantly, I am burning bridges to the past, all the while noticing, as if in penance, that the ideas and abilities of a trained pedant follow close as shadows.

A passage from an obscure journal by the philosopher Nelson Goodman often occupies my mind. "For me, there is no way which is the way the world is; and so of course no description can capture it. But there are many ways the world is, and every true description captures one of them." [12]

The universe we can know is a universe of descriptions. If we find we live in a moral vacuum, and if we believe this is due in part to economic language, then we are obligated to create alternatives to economic language. Old ways of seeing do not change because of evidence; they change because a new language captures the imagination. The progressive branches of environmentalism — defined by an implacable insistence on biodiversity, wilderness, and the replacement of our current social grid with bioregions — have been sloughing off old ideas and creating one of many possible new languages.

Emerson started the tradition by dumping his Unitarian vocabulary and writing "Nature" in language that restored nature's sacredness. Thoreau altered that vocabulary further and captured our imagination. The process continues with the labor of poets, deep ecologists, and naturalists. It is not limited to radical environmentalism, however; it includes many who are only partially sympathetic to the radical cause. Michael Pollan, for example, tells us in Second Nature that science has proposed some new descriptions of trees as the lungs of the Earth. And radical economist Thomas Michael Power suggests in The Economic Pursuit of Quality that "economy" might be extended beyond commerce. The process is enforced when Charles F. Wilkinson, in The Eagle Bird, suggests changes in the language of law that would honor our surrender to the beauty of the world and of emotion.

Imagine extending the common in "common good" to what is common to all life—the air, the atmosphere, the water, the processes of evolution and diversity, the commonality of all organisms in their common heritage. Imagine extending "community" to include all the life forms of the place that is your home. Imagine "accounting" in its original sense: *to be accountable.* What does it mean to be accountable, and to whom and to what purpose? What's "a good deal" with the Universe? Imagine an economics of need. Instead of asking "What is this worth?" ask "What does this forest need?" "What does this river need?"

Consider Lewis Hyde's beautiful description of an Amish quilt sale: "A length of rope stretched around the farm yard full of household goods. A little sign explained that it was a private auction, in which only members of the Amish community were allowed to bid. Though goods changed hands, none left the community. And none could be inflated in value. If sold on the open market, an old Amish quilt might be too valuable for a young Amish couple to sleep under, but inside that simple fence it would always hold its value on a winter night." [13]

"Hold its value on a winter night"? What's happening here?

It's as simple as that rope and a group of people deciding to place aspects of their shared experience above economic values determined by the open market. They don't ignore economic value—there is still a price, bidding, and competition—but it is restrained by a consensus of appreciation a wider market would ignore.

Although this example comes from a religious community, its power does not turn on religion; although it comes from an agricultural community, it does not turn on agriculture. It turns on two things: shared experience and shared place—the politics of locale. As does the Bill of Rights, the rope creates a limit with standards and values shared by the community. We need to imagine an immense fugue of variations on that simple fence, each creating a new world.

These imaginings will be the worthy labor of poets and thinkers and artists whose primary task, it seems to me, is to extend those qualities we value most deeply—the source of our moralities and spiritual practices—into what we call "the world." Many will find that source is empty, drained like the great aquifers that water our greed. Others will discover links between their integrity and that of an ecosystem, between their dignity and the dignity of a tree, between their desire for autonomy and the autonomy all beings desire, between their passions and the wild processes that sustain all life.

Extend these moral and spiritual sources into nature and the spirits of each treasured place will *speak* as they have always spoken — through art, myth, dreams, dance, literature, poetry, craft. Open the door and they will transform your mind — instantly. If children were raised hearing stories of spotted owls, honoring them with dances, imagining them in dreams, and seeking the power of their gaze, then spotted owls would speak to us, transformed by mind into *Our-Form-of-Life-At-The-Place-of-Spotted-Owls*.

Then we wouldn't have to worry about clear-cutting spotted-owl habitat. And when wildfires articulated their needs, we would not drown them in chemicals. When wild rivers spoke, they would be cleared of dams, and the salmon would come home from the sea.

Dig in someplace — like a great fir driving roots deep into a rocky ridge to weather storms that are inseparable from the shape of its roots. Allow the spirits of your chosen place to speak through you. Say their names. Say Moose Ponds, Teewinot, Pingora, Gros Ventre, Stewart Draw, Lost River. Speak of individuals — the pine marten that lives in the dumpster, the *draba* on the south ridge of the Grand Teton. Force the spirits of your place to be heard. Be hopeful. Language changes and imagination is on our side. Perhaps in a thousand years our most sacred objects will be illuminated floras, vast taxonomies of insects, and a repertoire of songs we shall sing to whales.

It is April and still cool beside Deer Creek in the Escalante country. Around me lies last year's growth, old sedges and grasses in lovely shades of umber and sienna. Beside me stands an ancient Fremont cottonwood. At the tips of its most extended and fragile branches, bright against a cobalt sky, are the crisp green buds of spring.

5

The Song of the White Pelican

I am a pelican of the wilderness. — Psalms

I am lounging on the summit of the Grand Teton surrounded by blocks of quartz and a cobalt sky. It is mid-morning in July — warm, still, and so clear the distant ranges seem etched into the horizon. To the east, the Absaroka, Gros Ventre, and Wind River; to the south, the Salt, Snake, and Caribou; to the west the Big Hole and the Lost River; and to the north, the Centennial, Madison, Gallatin, and Beartooth. Directly north, and closer, is the still-snowy summit of the Pitchstone Plateau, and beyond it the fuzzy blur of a geyser somewhere near Old Faithful. To the northeast are slices of Yellowstone Lake.

Despite the breadth of view I always feel this summit is a place of great simplicity. I have just climbed the Exum, or south, ridge of the Grand Teton with clients. They are taking photographs. Since I have climbed the Grand for thirty years, I have my pictures, and since I am fifteen years older than my oldest client, I am tired. So I rest and enjoy the clarity and count shades of blue as the sky pales into the mountains. Then I hear a faint noise above me, and my heart says, "Pelicans."

The sounds are faint, so faint they are sometimes lost — a trace of clacking in the sky. It is even harder to see them. Tiny glints, like slivers of ice, are occasionally visible, then invisible, then visible again as the sheen of their feathers strikes just the right angle to the sun. With binoculars we see them clearly: seventeen white pelicans soaring in a tight circle. I have seen them here before, as well as from the summit of Symmetry Spire and from the long ridge of

Rendezvous Peak. But it is rare — in part, I think, because the conditions for hearing and seeing them are so rare. Perhaps they are often above us, but with the wind and clouds and the ever-present anxiety of climbing, we fail to notice them.

The white pelican (*Pelecanus erythrorhynchos*), one of seven species in the world, is a large bird often weighing twenty pounds, with some individuals reaching thirty pounds. The only other pelican in North American, the brown pelican (*Pelecanus occidentalis*), is smaller and restricted to the coasts. The white pelican's wingspan reaches nine and a half feet, equal to the California condor's. Of North American birds, only the trumpeter swan is consistently larger.

Though huge, a pelican, like all birds, consists mostly of feathers, flesh, and air. The beak, skull, feet, and bones of a twenty-five-pound pelican weigh but twenty-three ounces. Its plumage is brilliant white except for the black primaries and outer secondaries, and pale yellow plumes on the crown of the head during breeding season. Occasionally there is pale yellow on the chest. Their eyes are the color of fine slate.

The summit of the Grand Teton is 13,770 feet high, and the pelicans above us are at the limit of unaided human vision. Since in good light a flock of white pelicans is easily visible at a mile, these pelicans are at least a mile above us, or higher than 19,000 feet. This seems high for any bird, but geese have been photographed at 29,000 feet, ravens are a nuisance on the South Col of Everest at 26,000 feet, and I have watched flocks of Brahminy ducks from Siberia cross the ridge between Everest and Cho Oyu, which is 19,500 feet at its low point. So although 19,000 feet is impressive, and no one knows how high pelicans can or do fly, the more interesting question is this: What are they *doing* up there? Soaring. Clacking. Yes, but why? I don't think anybody knows, and this mystery, along with the inevitable speculations, are a large part of why I find them so appealing.

For years I asked biologists and birders about pelican sounds, and they are unanimous: they have never heard a pelican make a sound. The popular bird books do not mention pelican sounds, and most of the technical literature reports that pelicans are mute except when breeding. Then the authors go on to admit they have spent little time around breeding pelicans. There are, of course, good reasons for this. The white pelican so dislikes human presence during breeding season that if approached, they will abandon their nests and raft on nearby water. The eggs, or chicks, are then exposed to the sun, to cold, and to the depredations of the ever-present gulls. An hour, or less, is sufficient to wipe out the breeding colony. If repeatedly harassed, white pelicans will abandon a rookery forever. For these reasons, monitoring the white pelican population is usually done from airplanes, increasingly with aerial photography. In one sense this is commendable, but in another it is sad, for fewer and fewer people know less and less about pelicans. The hard data are known—the average length of the bill, the average time of arrival and departure during migration, the average number of eggs—and no doubt will increase, but our understanding of pelicans, a way of knowing that requires intimacy, is nil.

We could, of course, let pelicans come to us. This is the difference between seeking and stalking and just sitting and waiting. It is an old difference, as old as hunting, but a difference that is hard for us to choose because we are, as a nation and as a civilization, a people of seeking and stalking, though exactly why this is so remains fugitive.

I used to visit an old Sherpa in Khumbu who had served on perhaps fifty Himalayan expeditions. His name was Dawa Tensing and he lived in a village just north of Thyangboche Monastery on the trail to Everest. He was famous for saying, "So many people coming, coming, always looking, never finding, always coming back again. Why?" Once, in all sincerity, he asked me: "Is America beautiful? Why you always come back here?"

It took a long time for Dawa's "Why?" to sink into my thick skull, and it took even longer to prefer his question to the closure of an answer. I suspect now that if we wish to know pelicans intimately, we must begin with a preference for questions and a preference for sitting and waiting. Perhaps it would be better if ornithologists were to become glider pilots, mountaineers, and fishermen, flying in the thermals, lounging atop great peaks, fishing great rivers, and waiting for pelicans to come to them.

If we sit quietly in the places of pelicans, I believe they *will* come to us. I have been sitting in a cabin in a national park for portions of sixteen years now. Although I do not feed wild animals, the eagles come and watch me from a nearby snag, a red squirrel sits by my elbow while I shave, martens and weasels look in my window, and deer and elk nip the weeds by the porch. Moose sometimes sleep on the porch — and scare the wits out of me when I go out at night to pee.

Dōgen's famous lines in the *Genjo Koan* are always suggestive, even when removed from their spiritual context:

> That the self advances and confirms the ten thousand things
> is called delusion;
> That the ten thousand things advance and confirm the self is
> enlightenment.[1]

The Japanese word here translated as "enlightenment" can also be translated as "intimacy." Perhaps it is time to realize that the knowledge won from hard data is limited; perhaps it is time to allow wild animals to establish the degree of intimacy between us. No radio collars, no netting, no banding, no intrusion into their lives. We wait; they decide.

A few people have spent time sitting with pelicans. In 1962 George Schaller spent 367 hours sitting in a canoe watching pelicans breed.[2] He heard lots of sounds. Others researchers have noted that pelicans hiss when angry, snap their mandibles together as a warning, and while mating make sounds that have been variously described as piglike or low-toned grunts, subdued croaking, a deep-voiced, murmuring groan, and grunting quacks. Audubon said they made a sound like blowing through the bunghole of a cask.

Although pelicans do make sounds, they are, relative to other birds, quite silent. There may be phylogenetic reasons for this. The newer species of birds are the most vocal and produce the greatest variety of sounds, while pelicans are very old — they've been around thirty-five to forty million years. We have one fossil record from the Pliocene, and we know they have been in the American West since the Pleistocene. Ornithologists have discovered prehistoric nesting sites on mountains that were once islands raising from the Pleistocene lakes that covered much of the Great Basin.

The silence of pelicans, along with their great age, contributes to their dignity. And this is no doubt augmented by the fact that the pelican is not a popular bird. The Hamilton stores in Yellowstone offer no pelican postcards or posters or stuffed pelicans or pelican candles or pelican-shaped coffee mugs — the kind of merchandise that nibbles at the dignity of other animals.

The white pelican, in short, is a quiet, dignified bird. The ones in

Yellowstone are also friendly. Although biologists stress that pelicans are always in flocks (except for stragglers during migration), and that they are timid, anyone who fishes Yellowstone knows that they are often solitary, sort of like fly fishermen; and after fishing Yellowstone's waters for thirty-three years, I believe that white pelicans are fond of their fishing kin. Their reason is probably a good pelican reason, a sustained meditation on "anything that spends that much time trying to catch trout can't be all bad." For although other pelicans eat rough fish, especially carp, 98 to 100 percent of a Yellowstone pelican's diet is *Salmo clarki lewisi,* otherwise known as the black-spotted trout or, more formally, as the westslope cutthroat. On my off days I am consoled by the firm belief that the karma of those who subsist on trout is superior to those who subsist on carp.

Still, there must be a touch of condescension in the birds' view of fly fishermen. Pelicans have been observed struggling with twenty-four-inch trout, and they are sometimes so bloated by success they have to vomit so they can lose enough weight to fly. On an average day, a Yellowstone pelican will eat more than four pounds of cutthroats. If the average fly fisherman had to catch four pounds of trout a day to survive, there would be fewer *Homo sapiens* than pelicans — and lots of carcasses surrounded by three thousand dollars worth of high-tech fishing gear.

Unlike the brown pelican, the white pelican does not dive for fish. It fishes with its bill and the flabby, stretchy gular pouch that hangs beneath it. The pelican is very clever with this pouch, using it as a dip net to catch fish, fluttering it to cool off (it is filled with blood vessels), and in one instance of a pelican in captivity, catching balls with it and throwing them back up into the air. Since its bill is about a foot long, the pelican must feed near the surface of the water, probably the top two or three feet. In deep water a group of pelicans will form a semicircle and by thrashing their wings and generally creating chaos drive fish into shallow water where they can reach them. But if fishing alone on a river, the pelican is attracted to fish feeding near the surface, and that means fish that are feeding on emerging aquatic insects and hatches.

The Yellowstone River is a great dry-fly river — what better place for a bird that must feed near the surface? If you go to the estuary below the lake during the gray drake mayfly hatch in late July, you will occasionally see pelicans floating amidst a blizzard of fly lines and mayflies, and performing upstream and downstream ferries like skilled kayakers to avoid all the people standing in the river. The novice fishermen are trying to match the huge duns, the pelicans and their followers are attending to the spinner fall.

Buffalo Ford, a picnic area with a small island offshore that divides the river and provides good holding water for trout, is another favorite place of pelican and fishermen. I have seen pelicans work this water just like an angler works a dry fly or an emerger. They land above the good water and float into the deep pool at the head of the island, then alongside the deep trench of the main current that flows between the east side of the island and the far shore; after reaching the tailwater below the island, they lift off and fly back to the head of the good water. Then they do this again and again—just like the rest of the folks fishing the ford.

But every time they land on the river, it looks like a disaster. They drop the backs of their huge wings, throw out their feet like wheels, and land with a controlled crash—like a 747. Every time, they almost nose over; every time, they just make it. Then, to regain their composure, they tuck their bills into their chests with that snotty, satisfied-English-butler look and casually paddle off after more trout, buoyant as a well-greased fly. As the poet Onitsura says,

> The water-bird
> Looks heavy,—
> But it floats![3]

Because I guide in the Tetons all summer, I have little time for fishing, but when work slows, I fish the Yellowstone River and, afterward, on my way home, I stop at the Lake Hotel. I tell myself it is for dinner, but this is just an excuse to sit in the lounge, listen to the string quartet that plays during the summer months, and watch the light on Yellowstone Lake. The owners recently repainted the lounge in civilized pale green, rose, mauve, and cream. I like to sit in a wicker wing chair, drink margaritas, and listen to music that does not remind me of machines. Last year the first violinist was a young woman who played beautifully. Her skin was a color found only inside seashells. Bent to her violin, she swayed in oblivion, concealed in the solitude of her music, fully present, but lost, as luminous and self-contained and remote as a star.

Just visible above her shoulder, through the bay windows at the end of the lounge, was the lake, speckled with whitecaps. In the distance stretched its southeast arm. The slant of evening light and the ever-present storm clouds darkened its western shore, while sunlight revealed light rock or fresh snow on the peaks of the Absaroka. Farther, almost concealed by clouds, were Colter Peak, Turret Peak, the Trident, the Two-Ocean Plateau. Farther still was the Thorofare, the wildest, most remote place in the lower forty-eight states.

At the tip of this southeast arm, just west of where the Yellowstone River enters the lake, and roughly a half mile off the western and southern shores, are the Molly Islands. If you were to stand on the shore, you would see two spits of sand named Sandy Island and Rocky Island. They are small, low, and sparsely dappled with Scouler willow, nettles, sky pilot, and cinquefoil. Until recently these remote islands were the only white pelican rookery in Wyoming, the chosen home of strange white birds thirty-five million years old.

The sweep of all this pleases me—the wing chair, the cold tequila, the precision of the music, the woman's passion for her violin, the view into that wildest place. It reminds me why, unlike some of my more radical environmental friends, I do not wish to return to the Pleistocene.

The first sighting of a white pelican in Yellowstone was reported by the Stuart party in 1863. Like good Americans they promptly shot one near what is now Pelican Creek. This set the tone for our relations with white pelicans for the next century. The population was nearly wiped out in the late twenties when it was discovered that the pelican carried a parasite that infected cutthroat trout. This, in addition to their high consumption of trout, led to the their slaughter. It was not an isolated act of stupidity. In 1918 the Utah Department of Fish and Game went to Hat Island, which was then a major breeding colony in the Great Salt Lake, and clubbed and shot hundreds of pelicans and herons.

The slaughter of pelicans fifty years ago is one reason we don't see more of them, and why the species is vulnerable. Another reason is the loss of habitat. Of the twenty-three breeding colonies in the American West, only five major sites remain. Many, like the Molly Islands, are small. In 1980 there were only 285 nests on the Molly Islands, and, unfortunately, the islands are so low they are vulnerable to flooding. According to the topographic map, Sandy

Island is only 6 feet above the lake and Rocky Island is only 9. When Schaller studied the colony in 1962, the lake rose 2.3 feet in June from a heavy snow pack and wiped out at least 80 pelican nests. It is conceivable that a heavier runoff would flood the islands and cause the pelicans to abandon the colony. That there are more than 100,000 breeding White Pelicans in North America would not diminish our loss.

For years there has been an effort to have the white pelican listed as endangered. The U.S. population is vulnerable, especially in Wyoming, where the white pelican is listed as a "Priority 1 species," one needing "immediate attention and active management to ensure that extirpation or a significant decline in the breeding population" does not occur.

On the Molly Islands, pelican chicks hatch when the bison calves drop. (They are exceptionally ugly: nothing looks so like a dinosaur as a pelican chick.) Soon thereafter, in a striking example of natural timing, the shallow streams around Yellowstone Lake become choked with spawning cutthroats laying billions of eggs in pelican-heaven water. Trout eat the unprotected eggs of other trout, larger trout eat little trout, and all of them are gobbled up by grizzlies, California gulls, and pelicans in a wild frenzy of gluttony and sex. It's a good time to be a pelican chick.

After ten or eleven weeks the chicks begin to fly, and soon afterwards they must become aware of the Teton range fifty miles to the southwest and clearly visible from above the southeast arm of Yellowstone Lake. From this direction the so-called Cathedral Group of peaks—Teewinot, Mount Owen, and the Grand Teton—resembles a pyramid. If you were a soaring bird, you would want to go there, and the white pelican is a soaring bird par excellence. Like the great pelagic wanderers, pelicans have wings with a high ratio of length to width. They are built to soar and they soar well—thirty-five million years of constant feedback and fine-tuned design make a difference. Anyone writing on pelicans mentions their soaring, and most have watched them disappear into the blue—the phrase usually used is some variation of "at the limit of human vision."

Of all places available to pelicans, mountains provide the most opportunities for soaring. Where the prevailing wind meets a mountain, it flows over it like water over a boulder in a rapid. Just as beyond the boulder is a hole followed by smaller standing waves, so there are standing "wave trains" of air currents beyond the mountain, and pelicans can soar up each one. Since our prevailing summer wind is from the southwest, the wave trains behind the Grand Teton point straight toward the Molly Islands.

Pelicans can also soar in thermals. As the ground warms, patches of warmer air rise, puff out at the top, peel off, and are sucked back into the vortex that keeps rising again and again through the center of the thermal. The stronger the rise, the stronger the thermal, and the tighter the circle a soaring bird can cut. The Teton range has strong thermals, and the pelicans above the Grand Teton always soar in tight circles, carving into the wind for lift, then dropping around for the tailwind, then farther around and into the wind again for more lift. Thermals tend to stack up in a long "thermal street" and drift downwind, allowing a pelican to climb in one thermal, cut out and glide to the next, climb again, cut out again—all with virtually no expenditure of energy. In the summer, the Grand Teton's thermals stack up in a line heading toward the Molly Islands.

Pelicans also soar in thunderheads, which suck cold air down from the upper atmosphere. When it hits the ground, it spreads out, displacing warmer air which, in turn, goes upward, creating more good soaring places. The Grand Teton has some of the most dazzling thunderstorms of any place on the planet, with lightning to match. During the most intense period of one recent storm, lightning struck every two minutes, and the storm lasted sixteen hours. Pelicans often wander the edges of great storms and I envy them this freedom, even with its risks. In one account, thirty-three pelicans were knocked out of the air by lightning in Nebraska. In a storm in Utah, twenty-seven were killed. The same thing must happen over the Tetons.

Ten years ago my guided party was hit four times by ground currents while descending the Grand Teton. We watched green bolts of lightning ricochet through glaciers like bullets. Yet I still climb mountains, and pelicans still soar in thunderheads. After thirty-five million years, they must know about lightning and its risks, just as mountaineers do, but it no more changes their behavior than it changes ours.

So there are many good reasons for the pelicans to be above the Grand Teton, but exactly why remains a mystery. The pelicans we see there in July are not migrating. Yellowstone pelicans winter in

Mexico and the Sea of Cortéz. Then in late March or early April they fly to the Great Salt Lake. In late April or early May they fly to the Molly Islands. Perhaps the pelicans over the Grand Teton in July are returning from a foraging mission. Perhaps they are non-breeding adults on a lark. Perhaps someone will put a radio collar on one and find out, though I hope not. Whatever science would discover is not worth the intrusion into their wild lives. What interests me is not that pelicans can soar, that soaring is useful, or that they soar here. What interests me is the question of whether pelicans love to soar.

The pelican's love of soaring is only hinted at in ornithological literature, but it is there. In his *Handbook of North American Birds*, volume one, Ralf Palmer uses the word "indulge" in the cryptic grammar of scientific description. He says the pelicans "often indulge in high-soaring flights" and that "while soaring in stormy weather [they] may indulge in aerial acrobatics with much swooping and diving" (270). This is not exactly the language of mechanistic science. Does this mean that pelicans are, sometimes at least, soaring for pleasure? Do they play in thunderheads for fun? Do they fly in thunderheads knowing full well the danger? Do they experience ecstasy while soaring so indulgently? What could it mean to attribute these emotions to a bird?

Consider Doug Peacock's film footage of the grizzly he named Happy Bear.[4] In the spring, when the streams are still frozen, Happy Bear likes to sit on his butt in small meadow streams and break off chunks of ice, bite them, push them underwater with his huge paws, then bite them again when they pop up. He does this a lot. I don't think we can say why Happy Bear is doing this without using analogies and metaphors from human emotional life.

Or consider the gulls in Guy Murchie's *Song of the Sky:*

Many a time I have seen sea gulls at the big Travis Air Base near San Francisco flapping nonchalantly among the huge ten-engined B-36 bombers while their motors were being run up. The smoke whipping from the jets in four straight lines past the tail accompanied by that soul-shaking roar would have been enough to stampede a herd of elephants but the sea gulls often flew right into the tornado just for fun. When the full blast struck them they would simply disappear, only to turn up a few seconds later a quarter mile downwind, apparently having enjoyed the experience as much as a boy running through a hose — even coming around eager-eyed for more.[5]

Simply disappear. Like paddling a kayak into Lava Falls.

It is not popular now to attribute human characteristics and processes to wild animals, since it projects onto the Other our biases and perceptions and limits our view of their difference. But all description is merely analogy and metaphor, and as such is forever imperfect and respectful of mystery. We are more ignorant and limited than we can conceive. Even scientific descriptions and theories are contingent and subject to revision. We do not understand even our dog or cat, not to mention a vole. Even our knowledge of those we know best — our lovers and friends — is fragile and often mistaken. Our knowledge of strangers in our own culture is even more fragile, and it seems that despite our volumes of social science, we have no understanding of native peoples. Language may probe the mystery of the Other, but the Other remains a mystery.

We also fail to appreciate that many of our descriptions and explanations of human behavior are appropriations from wild animals: the lion-hearted hero, the wolfish cad, the foxy lady. And this suggests that life is a spectrum where unity is more pervasive than difference — a rudimentary truth for the Apache and the Bushman, but a truth ignored by our epistemologies.

It is no more odd to say that pelicans love to soar and do so in *ecstasy* than it is to say what we so commonly say of human love and ecstasy: that our heart soars. Or, to take another example, to describe meditation as Dōgen does in the *Mountains and Rivers Sutra:* "Because mountains are high and broad, the way of riding the clouds is always reached in the mountains; the inconceivable power of soaring in the wind comes freely from the mountains."[6]

Some people fear that extending a human vocabulary to wild animals erodes their Otherness. But what is *not Other?* Are we not all, from one perspective, Other to each and every being in the universe? And at the same time, and from another perspective, do we not all share an elemental wildness that burns forth in each life?

When I see white pelicans riding mountain thermals, I feel their exaltation, their love of open sky and big clouds. Their fear of lightning is my fear, and I extend to them the sadness of descent. I believe the reasons they are soaring over the Grand Teton are not so different from the reasons we climb mountains, sail gliders into great storms, and stand in rivers with tiny pieces of feathers from a French duck's butt attached to a barbless hook at the end of sixty feet of a sixty-dollar string thrown by a thousand-dollar wand. Indeed, in love and ecstasy we are closest to the Other, for passion is at the root of all life and shared by all life. In passion, all beings are at their wildest; in passion, we—like pelicans—make strange noises that defy scientific explanation.

If pelicans are soaring above the Grand Teton in ecstasy, how should we describe their clacking? I can find only one reference in our immense literature on birds to the clacking that pelicans make at high altitude. In his *Life Histories of North American Petrels and Pelicans and Their Allies,* Arthur Cleveland Bent quotes Dr. P. L. Hatch as saying, "This immense bird usually signals his arrival in the early part of April by his characteristic notes from an elevation beyond the range of vision except under the most favorable circumstances. The sound of those notes is difficult to describe, but unforgettable when once certainly heard from their aerial heights" (291). Why do they utter that unforgettable sound only when they are so far up in the sky—at the limit of our vision? Olaus Murie once said of the coyote's howl that "if the coyote could reflect and speak he would say this is his song, simply that."[7] Simply that: the song of coyote. All things have their song, and few questions about songs have answers.

I believe the clacking in the sky over the Grand Teton is the song of the white pelican. I believe they sing their song in ecstasy, from joy in an experience unique to their perfections. I know climbers who whistle, sing, and yodel when they are up in the sky. William Blake died singing to the angels he knew were leading him to heaven. Some sing, some whistle, some yip, some clack in the sky, some make love to a violin. Why saw at strings of gut stretched over holes in burnished wood? Why sing cantatas and masses and chorales?

All life contains its anguish, even a trout-eating pelican's life—the Buddha's first noble truth. But all life must occasionally experience a release. In passion and ecstasy, all life lets go—of what?

6

In Wildness Is the Preservation
of the World

I wish my neighbors were wilder. — Henry Thoreau

Hanging from the ceiling of the visitors center at Point Reyes National Seashore are plaques bearing famous quotations about the value of the natural world. The one from Thoreau, from his essay "Walking," reads: "In Wilderness is the preservation of the World." This, of course, is a mistake. Henry didn't say "wilderness," he said "wildness." But the mistake has become a cliché, suitable for T-shirts and bumper stickers. I think this mistake is like a Freudian slip: it serves a repressive function, the avoidance of conflict, in this case the tension between wilderness as property and wildness as quality. I also think we are all confused about this tension. William Kittredge has been candid enough to admit that "For decades I misread Thoreau. I assumed he was saying wilderness. . . . Maybe I didn't want Thoreau to have said wildness, I couldn't figure out what he meant."[1] I agree.

I believe that mistaking wilderness for wildness is one cause of our increasing failure to preserve the wild earth and that Kittredge's honesty identifies the key issue: we are confused about what Thoreau meant by wildness, we aren't sure what we mean by wildness, and we aren't clear how or what wildness preserves.

If you study the indexes in the recent scholarly edition of Thoreau's works published by Princeton University Press, you will discover that "wild" and "wilderness" do not often occur. Nor do Thoreau's journal entries during the period he was writing "Walking," roughly the spring of 1851, explain what he might have meant. But after reading Richard C. Trench's *On the Study of Words*, published in 1852, Thoreau made the following important note in his "Fact-Book": "*Wild*—past particle of *to will*, self-willed."[2]

We are also confused about what Thoreau meant by "world." I do not believe he meant merely our planet, even in the fashionable sense of Gaia. Near the end of "Walking" he says, "We have to be told that the Greeks called the world Κόσμος, Beauty, or Order, but we do not see clearly why they did so, and we esteem it at best only a curious philological fact."[3] Our modern word is *cosmos*, and the most recent philological studies suggest the meaning of harmonious order.[4] So in the broadest sense we can say that Thoreau's "In Wildness is the preservation of the World" is about the relation of free, self-willed, and self-determinate "things" with the harmonious order of the cosmos. Thoreau claims that the first preserves the second. The problem is this: it is not clear to any of us, I think, how the wildest acts of nature—earthquakes, wildfires, the plagues, people being killed and eaten by mountain lions and grizzly bears, our lust, the open sea in storm—preserve a harmonious cosmic order.

I know of no author who directly addresses this issue, and a cursory examination of our environmental literature will convince anyone that we are not dealing with a saying that, for most preservationists, describes the heart of our ideology. Indeed, it was not until Gary Snyder published *The Practice of the Wild* that we had a general discussion of what nature, wildness, and wilderness mean and how they are connected. This situation shouldn't surprise us, because most people no longer have much direct experience of wild nature, and few meditate on the cosmos. Since language and communication are social phenomena that presume common, shared experience, it follows that clarity about the issue, perhaps even discourse, is impossible. I would go so far as to say that in many inner cities, here and in the developing world, people no longer have a concept of wild nature based on personal experience. Mostly, the wild is something bad reported by television. As a New York wit has it, "Nature is something I pass through between my hotel and my taxi." And, needless to say, a growing world population ignorant of the key concepts of our movement will hinder the cause of preservation and render its goals increasingly unrealistic.

"Walking," and also *Walden* and two other essays—"Resistance to Civil Government" (unfortunately called "Civil Disobedience" most of the time) and "Life without Principle"—express the radical heart of Thoreau's life's work, and since he revised "Walking" just before his death, we may assume it accurately represents his ideas.

The most notable fact about these works is that Thoreau virtually ignores our current concerns with the preservation of habitats and species. He would no doubt include them—he says "all good things are wild and free"—but he writes mainly about human beings, their literature, their myths, their history, their work and leisure, and, of course, their walking. His question, which he got from Emerson, is about human life: "How ought I to live?" Thoreau is unique because part of his answer to this old question involves wildness. In "Walking," he says, for instance, "Give me for my friends and neighbors wild men, not tame ones. The wildness of the savage is but a faint symbol of the awful ferity with which good men and lovers meet" (122). And listen to the essay's opening lines: "I wish to speak a word for Nature, for absolute freedom and wildness, as contrasted with a freedom and culture merely civil, —to regard man as an inhabitant, or a part and parcel of Nature, rather than a member of society" (93). Absolute freedom. Absolute wildness. Human beings as inhabitants of that absolute freedom and wildness. This is not the usual environmental rhetoric, and Kittredge is surely correct: most of us simply don't know what Thoreau means.

What is equally confounding is that people who have led a life of intimate contact with wild nature—a buckaroo working the Owyhee country, a halibut fisherman plying the currents of the Gulf of Alaska, an Eskimo whale hunter, a rancher tending a small cow/calf operation, a logger with his chain saw—often oppose preserving wild nature. The friends of preservation, on the other hand, are often city folk who depend on weekends and vacations in designated wilderness areas and national parks for their (necessarily) limited experience of wildness. This difference in degree of experience of wild nature, the dichotomy of friends/enemies of preservation, and the notorious inability of these two groups to communicate also indicate the depth of our muddle about wildness. We don't know what we mean, and those who have the most experience with the wild disagree with what we want to achieve.

We also presume that the experience of wildness and wilderness are related, and this is plausible (though it ignores elements of our personal lives that also might be thought of as wild: sex, dreams, rage, etc.). However, since wilderness is a place, and wildness a quality, we can always ask, "How wild is our wilderness?" and "How wild is our experience there?" My answer? Not much, particularly in the wilderness most people are familiar with, the areas protected by the Wilderness Act of 1964.

There are many reasons for this. Some are widely acknowledged, and I will pass over them briefly, but there is one reason that is not widely accepted, a reason that is offensive to many minds, but one that goes to the heart of Thoreau's opening lines, namely, that human beings no longer accept their status as "part and parcel" of a biological realm that is self-willed, self-determined, self-ordered. Instead we have divided ourselves from that realm and make every attempt to control it for our own interests. Wilderness is one of the few places where we can begin to correct this division; hence, despite the rage for wilderness as a bastion for conserving bio-diversity, I am inclined to think its primary importance remains what the founders of the conservation movement thought it was: a basis for an important kind of human experience. Without big, wild wilderness I doubt most of us will ever see ourselves as part and parcel of nature.

Why isn't our wilderness wild, and why is there so little experience of wildness there? Well, first of all, the wilderness that most people visit (with the exception of Alaska and Canada) is too small — in space and time. Like all experience, the experience of the wild can be a taste or a feast, and a feast presumes substance and leisure. Yet about a third of our legislated wilderness units are smaller than 10,000 acres, an area approximately four miles long on each side. An easy stroll. Some wilderness areas, usually islands, have fewer than 100 acres, and I have been told that Point Reyes now has meaningless "wilderness zones" measuring several hundred yards.

Even our largest wilderness areas are small. Only 4 percent are larger than 500,000 acres, an area 27 miles on a side, and since many follow the ridges of mountain ranges, they are so elongated that a strong hiker can cross one in a single day. True, some are adjacent to other wilderness areas and remote BLM lands and national parks, but compared to the Amazon, Alaska, the Northwest Territories, or the Himalayas, most Wilderness Act-wilderness seems very small indeed.

Unfortunately, without sufficient space and time the experience of wildness in the wilderness is diminished or simply doesn't exist. Many people agree with Aldo Leopold that it should take a couple of weeks to pack across a true wilderness, something that probably isn't possible in the lower forty-eight now. The law is simple: The farther you are from a road, and the longer you are out, the wilder your experience. Two weeks is the minimum, a month is better. Until then the mind remains saturated with human concerns and blind to the natural world, the body bound to metronomic time and ignorant of natural biological rhythms. A traveler in small wilderness for a weekend backpack trip remains ignorant of these differences between short and long stays in wilderness, yet a long stay is fundamental to seeing ourselves as part of biological nature, for the order of nature is above all a rhythmic order.

Second, small wilderness units usually lack predators. Sometimes this is simply a function of their small size, but sometimes it's a function of artificial borders created according to economic and political, rather than ecological, criteria. The result is the same: the wilderness is tamed. Predators are perhaps our most accessible experience of the wild. To come upon a grizzly track is to experience the wild in a most intimate, carnal way, an experience that is marked by gross alterations in attention, perception, body language, body chemistry, and emotion. Which is to say you feel yourself as part of the biological order known as the food chain, perhaps even as part of a meal.

Third, this tameness is exacerbated by our current model for appropriate human use of the wild—the intensive recreation that requires trail systems, bridges, signs for direction and distance, backcountry rangers, and rescue operations that in turn generate activities that further diminish wildness—maps, guide books, guiding services, advertising, photography books, instructional films—all of which diminish the discovery, surprise, the unknown, and the often-dangerous Other—the very qualities that make a place wild. Each of these reductions tames and domesticates the wilderness and diminishes wild experience.

Fourth, intensive recreational use influences public policy, leading those with authority to institute artificial methods of control that benefit recreational use. Animal populations are managed by controlled hunting, wildfires are suppressed, predators moved, and humans treated in a manner best described by the word "surveillance." The wild becomes a problem to be solved by further human intervention—scientific studies, state and federal laws, judicial decision, political compromise, and administrative and bureaucratic procedures. Once this intervention begins, it never ends; it spirals into further and further human intrusion, rendering wilderness increasingly evaluated, managed, regulated, and controlled. That is, tamed. Nibble by nibble, decision by decision, animal by animal, fire by fire, we have diminished the wildness of our wilderness.

Thus diminished, wilderness becomes a special unit of property treated like a historic relic or ruin—a valuable remnant. It becomes a place of vacations (a word related to "vacant, empty"). Humans become foreigners to the wild, foreigners to an experience that once grounded their most sacred beliefs and values. In short, wilderness as relic leads to tourism, and tourism in the wilderness becomes the primary mode of experiencing a diminished wild.

Wilderness as relic always converts places into commodities, because tourism, in its various manifestations, is a form of commerce. All tourism is to some degree destructive, and wilderness tourism is no exception. Virtually everyone (including me) in "the Nature business" feeds (literally) on wilderness as commodity. We are enthralled with our ability to make a living with this exchange, but we tend to ignore the practical consequences for wilderness preservation and for ourselves. Wilderness tourism is not a free lunch. Its worse consequence is that it conceals what should be its primary use: the wild as a project of the self. Compared with residency in a wild biological realm, where the experience of wildness is part of everyday life, wilderness tourism is pathetic. It has had some very bad consequences, and we need to acknowledge them.

Wilderness tourism ignores, perhaps even caricatures, the experience that decisively marked the founders of wilderness preservation: Henry Thoreau, John Muir, Robert Marshall, Aldo Leopold, and Olaus Murie. The kind of wildness they experienced has become very rare—an endangered experience. As a result, we no longer understand the roots of our own cause. Reading the works of these men and then looking at an issue of, say, *Sierra* can cause severe disorientation. The founders had something we lack, something Thoreau called "Indian Wisdom." For much of their lives these men lived in and studied nature before it became a "wilderness area," and their knowledge came not from visitor centers and guidebooks but from intimate, direct personal experience.

Thoreau's knowledge of the lands surrounding Concord was so vast that some of the town's children believed that, like God, Henry had created it all. His knowledge of flora was so precise, a rare fern species not seen for a hundred years was recently rediscovered by examining his notes, and his examination of the succession of forest trees is a seminal essay for modern ecology. Muir spent months alone in the wild Sierra Nevada and made original contributions to the study of glaciers. The lives of Marshall, Leopold, and Murie similarly exhibit extensive personal experience and knowledge of wilderness and wildness. To a considerable degree their lives were devotions to wild nature. Without such devotion, I do not believe there would be Thoreau's epiphanies on Katahdin, Muir's mystical identification with trees, or Leopold's thinking like a mountain.

Wilderness tourism is completely different. It is devoted to fun. We hunt for fun, fish for fun, climb for fun, ski for fun, and hike for fun. This is the grim harvest of the "fun hog" philosophy that powered the wilderness-recreation boom for three decades, the philosophy of *Outside* magazine and dozens of its ilk, and there is little evidence that either the spiritual or scientific concerns of the original conservationists — or the scientific concerns of conservation biologists — have trickled down to most wilderness fun hogs.

Given the ignorance and arrogance of most fun hogs, it is understandable that those who stand to lose by increased wilderness designation — farmers, ranchers, loggers, commercial fisherman, American Indians — are often enraged. Instead of a clash of needs, the preservation of the wild appears to be a clash of work versus recreation. Lacking a deeper experience of wildness and access to the lore, myth, metaphor, and ritual necessary to share that experience, there is no communication, no vision, that might shatter the current dead-end of wilderness debate. Both groups exploit the wild, the first by consuming it, the second by converting it into a playpen and then consuming it. Worship of wilderness designation thus becomes idolatry, the confusion of a symbol with its essence. In either case the result is the same: destruction of the wild.

With wilderness tourism we also lose our most effective weapon for preserving what little remains of the natural world: emotional identification. At the bedrock level, what drives both reform environmentalism and deep ecology is a practical problem: how to compel human beings to respect and care for wild nature. The tradition of Thoreau and Muir says that the best way to do this is raw, visceral contact with wild nature. True residency in the wild brings identification and a generalized "not in my back yard," or NIMBY, response that extends sympathy to all the wild world. Without this identification, solutions are abstract and impotent—that is, impractical. But because so many of us are obsessed with fun in the wild, there is a lot of impractical, impotent stuff dominating environmental thought. We have fun and we have philosophy, but we have little serious use of wilderness to study our place in nature, to study, that is, the relation between freedom and the cosmos.

For example, giving trees and animals moral rights analogous to the rights of humans has bogged down in a morass of value theory. The aesthetic campaign to preserve the wild has done as much harm as good, since it suggests (especially in a nation of relativists) that preservation is a matter of taste, a preference no more compelling than the choice between vanilla and chocolate. It leads to tedious arguments that begin with "Who are you to say that we shouldn't have snowmobiles in the Teton wilderness?" on the model of "Who are you to say I shouldn't eat chocolate?" This, in turn, leads inevitably to questions of egalitarianism and elitism, and hence directly into the dismal swamp of politics, which, as Thoreau says in "Walking," is the most alarming of man's affairs. Politicians are invariably people of the *polis*—city slickers, those furthest removed from the natural order.

Philosophers have been no more helpful. Deep ecologists are desperately attempting to replace the philosophical foundations of a mechanical model of the world with those of an organic model of the world. Unfortunately, these new foundations are not at all obvious to the other philosophers, not to mention the lay public. The search for foundations—for science, mathematics, logic, or the social sciences—has been the curse of rationalism from Descartes to the present, and the foundations of deep ecology will not exorcise that curse. Many explications of deep ecology rely on some of the most obscure ruminations of Spinoza, Whitehead, and Heidegger. This bodes ill for big wilderness.

All these things are reasonable (sort of), but as Hume saw clearly, reason alone is insufficient to move the will. We should repeat this to ourselves every day like a mantra. Reason has not compelled us to respect and care for wild nature, and we have no basis to believe it will in the future. Philosophical arguments, moralizing, aesthetics, political legislation, and abstract philosophies are notoriously incapable of compelling human behavior. Given the choice, I would side with the fun hogs, who are at least out there connecting with the wild on some level.

Wilderness tourism also results in little art, literature, poetry, myth, or lore for many, if not most, of our wild places. In "Walking," Thoreau described "the West" as "preparing to add its fables to those of the East. The valleys of the Ganges, the Nile, and the Rhine, having yielded their crop, it remains to be seen what the valleys of the Amazon, the Platte, the Orinoco, the St. Lawrence, and the Mississippi will produce" (121). Well, nearly 150 years later, it still remains to be seen. If you ask for the art, literature, lore, myth, and fable of where I live, the headwaters of the Snake River, I would answer that we are working on it, but it might be awhile, because art that takes a place as its subject is created by people who live in and develop a sense of that place. And this takes lots of time. This is true of both wilderness and civilization. Joyce grew up in Dublin, Atget lived in Paris, Muir and Adams lived in Yosemite, Henry Beston lived on Cape Cod. Many of our best writers on wilderness—Abbey, Snyder, Peacock—worked as fire lookouts for the U.S. Forest Service. (There is probably a doctoral dissertation here: "The Importance of Fire Lookouts in the Development of Western Nature Literature.") But if access to the wild world is limited to weekend tourism, we have no reason to expect a literature and lore of wild nature.

Yet most of us, when we think about it, realize that after our own direct experience of nature, what has contributed most to our love of wild places, animals, plants—and even, perhaps, to our love of wild nature, our sense of our citizenship—is the art, literature, myth, and lore of nature. For here is the language we so desperately lack, the medium necessary for vision. Mere concepts and abstractions will not do, because love is beyond concepts and abstractions. And yet the problem is one of love. As Stephen Jay Gould wrote, "We cannot win this battle to save species and environments without forging an emotional bond between ourselves and nature as well—for we will not fight to save what we do not love." [5] The conservation movement has put much thought, time, effort, and money into public policy and science, and far too little into direct personal experience and the arts. There is nothing wrong with public policy and science, but since they will not produce love, they must remain secondary in the cause of preservation.

And finally, wilderness tourism produces no phenology of wild places, the study of periodic phenomena in nature—bird migration, mating of animals, leafing of trees, the effects of climate. This is unfortunate, for phenology, as Paul Shepard has reminded us, is the study of the mature naturalist — the gate through which nature becomes personal.[6] Leopold published phenological studies of two counties in Wisconsin, and Thoreau dedicated the last years of his life to studying the mysterious comings and goings of the natural world. Phenology requires a complete immersion in place over time so that the attention, the senses, and the mind can scrutinize and discern widely — the dates of arrivals and departures, the births, the flourishings, the decays, and the deaths of wild things, their successions, synchronicities, dependencies, reciprocities, and cycles — the lived life of the earth. To be absorbed in this life is to merge with larger patterns. Here ecology is not studied, but felt, so that truths become known in the same way a child learns hot from cold — truths that are immune from doubt and argument and, most important, can never be taken away. Here is the common wisdom of indigenous peoples, a wisdom that cannot emerge from tourism in a relic wilderness.

We are left with the vital importance of residency in wild nature, and a visceral knowledge of that wildness, as the most practical means of preserving the wild. What we need now is a new tradition of the wild that teaches us how human beings live best by living in and studying the wild without taming it or destroying it. Such a tradition of the wild did exist; it is as old as the Pleistocene. Before Neolithic times, human beings were always living in, traveling through, and using lands we now call wilderness; they knew it intimately, they usually respected it, they often cared for it. It is the tradition of the people that populated all of the wilderness of North America, a tradition that influenced Taoism and Hinduism and informed major Chinese and Japanese poetic traditions. It is the tradition that emerged again with Emerson and Thoreau. In short, it is a tradition that could again compel respect, care, and love for wild nature in a way that philosophical foundations, aesthetics, moral theory, and public policy cannot. It is a tradition we need to re-create for ourselves, borrowing when necessary from native cultures, but making it new — a wild tradition of our own.

A wild bunch is forming, an eclectic tribe returning to the wild to study, learn, and express. From them will come the lore, myth, literature, art, and ritual we so require. Frank Craighead, John Haines, and Gary Snyder are among the elders of this tribe. There is also Richard Nelson on his island, Doug Peacock with his grizzlies, Terry Tempest Williams and her beloved birds, Hannah

Hinchman and her illuminated journals, Gary Nabhan and his seeds, Dolores LaChapelle and her rituals, and many others—all new teachers of the wild. Their mere presence is not sufficient, however. It will not help us if this tradition is created for us, to be read about in yet another book. To create a wilder self, the self must live the life of the wild, mold a particular form of human character, a form of life. Relics will not do, tourism will not do, books will not do.

If we want this wilder self, we must begin, in whatever ways we can imagine, to rejoin the natural world. One way is to consider our bodies as food for others. Out there is the great feeding mass of beings we call the Earth. We incorporate, and are incorporated, in ways not requiring legal papers. We are creator and created, terrorist and hostage, victim and executioner, guest of honor and part of the feast. This system of food, which is hidden from the urban mind, is terrifying in its identity and reciprocity. It is a vision that could inform everything from our private spiritual matters to the gross facts of nourishment and death. It at least partly answers Thoreau's question, "How should I live?" Now we have to figure out how we can achieve it here and now, in this place, in these times.

I am convinced that such a life is still possible. I love my Powerbook, my Goretex gear, and my plastic kayak. But I also make a point to eat fritillaria, morels, berries, fish, and elk. I want to feed directly from my place, to incorporate it. When I die, I wish my friends could present my body as a gift to the flora and fauna of my home, Grand Teton National Park, because I want my world to incorporate me.

On my travels in Tibet I was always delighted by the tradition of sky-burial. The human body is cut up and the bones broken to the marrow and left for animals, mostly birds. Later the bones are pounded and mixed with tsampa—a roasted barley—and again offered to the animals. Finally everything is gone, gone back into the cycle. Recently, when a friend lost her beloved dog, she carried it out to a beautiful view of the mountains, covered it with wild flowers, and left it for the coyotes and ravens and bugs. We should have the courage to do the same for ourselves, to re-enter the great cycle of feeding.

The moose incorporates the willow, taking the life of the willow into its own life, making the wildness of the willow reincarnate. I kill the moose, its body feeds the willow and grouse wortleberries where it dies, it feeds my body, and in feeding my body, the willow and the moose feed the one billion bacteria that inhabit three inches of my colon, the one million spirochetes that live in my mouth, and the microscopic brontosaurus-like mites that live by devouring the goo on my eyelashes. This great feeding body is the world. It evolved together, mutually, all interdependent, all interrelating ceaselessly, the dust of old stars hurtling through time, and we are the form it chose to make it conscious of itself.

From this vision of a wild order in complete interdependence comes freedom, a freedom unlike our civil freedoms but, I think, close to what Thoreau imagined. Perhaps it is best expressed by the Taittiriya Upanishad:[7]

> O wonderful! O wonderful! O wonderful!
> I am food! I am food! I am food!
> I eat food! I eat food! I eat food!
> My name never dies, never dies, never dies!
> I was born first in the first of the worlds,
> earlier than the gods, in the belly of what has no death!
> Whoever gives me away has helped me the most!
> I, who am food, eat the eater of food!
> I have overcome this world!
>
> He who knows this shines like the sun.
> Such are the laws of mystery!

7

The Importance of Peacock

Undoubtedly, all men are not equally fit subjects for
civilization; and because the majority, like dogs and sheep,
are tame by inherited disposition, this is no reason why the others
should have their natures broken that they may be reduced
to the same level. — Henry Thoreau

✳

Men went to Vietnam young. Those who returned were old, aged
by trauma and a reality so real their past lives were forever severed from their present. Once home they faced indifference, even
hostility. There were no parades and few heroes.

With the publication of Edward Abbey's *The Monkey Wrench
Gang* in 1975, one veteran, a former Green Beret, became one of
those heroes, not only to other veterans but to a nascent contingent of environmentalists who perceived themselves as radical. The
hero, depending on your views of fiction and reality, was either
George W. Hayduke, the novel's archetypal monkey wrencher, or
Abbey's model for Hayduke, his friend Doug Peacock. There is no
need to explain why Hayduke is a hero, but I want to explain why
Doug Peacock is one of my heroes.

Because Hayduke arrived in the public's imagination before the
real Peacock did, there was bound to be some confusion. Gary
Snyder suffered the same confusion as the model for Kerouac's
Jaffy Ryder in *Dharma Bums* and is quick to point out he is *not*
Jaffy Ryder. And although Gary Hemming is not alive to say so,
he is not the Rand of James Salter's novel *Solo Faces*.

Likewise, Peacock is not Hayduke, however much the public —
and sometimes Peacock — loves the association. Hayduke was a
caricature that allowed Abbey to indulge in some elaborate red-
neck posturing. Abbey studied philosophy and creative writing at
the universities of New Mexico, Yale, Edinburgh, and Stanford. In
Peacock's memoir *Grizzly Years*, we learn that he was doing gradu-

ate work in geology at the University of Michigan before the war, that he likes Mozart, can compare a friend to characters in Dostoyevsky, sees a burning pine as a burning bush, describes his nemesis — the Black Grizzly — as his Moby Dick, and is partial to expensive French wine. Abbey and Peacock were no more rednecks than they were Baptists.

Nor were they politicians. Neither believed in a life devoted to political causes, even though they were among the founders of Earth First!. The other founders of Earth First! were trained as, and have remained, environmental politicians. Peacock is not an environmentalist in any ordinary sense of the word, and he is anything but a politician.

The Monkey Wrench Gang is great fun as romantic fiction, but Hayduke remains stunted and pathetic — a warrior trapped in the old myth of destruction, unable to come in from the cold. True, he destroys for a good cause — he destroys the machines that are destroying the wild — but it is still destruction, and we suspect that like all destruction, its source is self-destruction; that he is less righteous than self-righteous, motivated less by an anger than by hate. One consequence of all this destruction is that Hayduke never heals from the trauma of war.

In contrast, Peacock didn't join the radical do-gooders, although he is said to have done some casual monkey wrenching (everyone needs a hobby) and in many ways served as a role model. But he didn't care enough about monkey wrenching to live up to the archetypal Hayduke. And he is clear about why: "Deep down I lacked any instinct for taking up causes, caring only about wild places and resurrecting a few of the dead."[1] Hayduke hates, Peacock cares. Hence unlike Hayduke, Peacock heals — somewhat.

Grizzly Years is not about destruction, but about how wilderness and wild animals might retrieve a soul. Since most of Peacock's healing came from grizzly bears — their main gift to him — it is little wonder that he loves them so. But another part of the healing came from his writing and later his film work, both expressions of the love he felt for — one wants to say "his" — grizzlies. These expressions initiated the elaborate feedback and reciprocity that make love potent. And among those most needing a potent love are grizzly bears and men traumatized by war.

I believe all men are defined for life by how they spent their twenties. Peacock is a writer trained as a warrior and a medic;

Abbey was a writer trained as a philosopher. Their apolitical stance is crucial to their influence. One *Monkey Wrench Gang* or *Grizzly Years* is worth a thousand monkey wrenchings. We can all drive a spike into a tree, but few can produce visionary fiction or memoirs that transform our beliefs and extend the possibilities of what we might come to love. To love *Ursus arctos horribilis,* North America's most formidable predator, requires either a firm philosophical stance or a warrior spirit. Probably both. That Peacock managed to love grizzlies and to form what can only be called relationships with some of them is as remarkable as it is singular, and the primary reason for his importance in the annals of preservation.

When Peacock returned from Vietnam after three consecutive tours of duty as a Green Beret, he bought a Jeep and drove west to his favorite wild haunts. In Vietnam he had carried a talisman, a tattered road map of Montana, to remind him of both beloved country and mythical place. So when Peacock drove west, he didn't just drive in a westerly direction, he headed for Thoreau's West — the West that is but another name for the Wild — and he went there for a reason: "Something was wrong. On the outside I was calm, even passive, but there was something frenzied on the inside." [2]

Sickened by the killing and destruction of war, he sought a different kind of challenge, one that embraced risk and its teachings without destroying the source of risk. For just as there is no cure without risk, there is no cure if you destroy the source of the risk. In short, Peacock required what is required of all seekers and wanderers — a mixture of danger and love. Like many who have endured a dark night of the soul, he headed into the wilderness and spent long periods of time there, often alone.

This is extremely rare in the culture of modernity. I am certain that less that one percent of our population has ever spent a day in truly wild country, and the number who have done so alone is infinitesimal. Can the citizens of modernity understand the values of a Muir or Peacock? Can they, to use modern parlance, understand the discourse? Yet if more people go into the wild to gain this understanding, will not their presence further undermine the wild? And why don't more do so? If wilderness is a tonic for the evils of civilization, the percentage taking the cure is diminishing exponentially with urbanization and the turn toward virtual reality. So Peacock is also important because *Grizzly Years* describes how wilderness can be a strong tonic for trauma. It is the story of a cure, a spiritual cure.

Going into the wild to be restored from the traumas of war is a tradition of sorts. After World War I, R. M. Patterson roamed the Nahanni River country of the Northwest Territories and wrote one of the classics of adventure literature, *The Dangerous River.* More recently another Vietnam veteran, James P. McMullen, went into the Everglades and wrote *Cry of the Panther.* There are many other examples. In *Across the Wide Missouri,* Bernard DeVoto speaks of "a type not uncommon after the Napoleonic wars, after all wars — men to whom campaigning and battle had been a climactic experience, giving them a sense of reality and function surpassing anything peace had to offer, convincing them that in extremity they had been most truly themselves, and leaving them to spend the rest of their lives looking for an experience, any kind of experience, that for even a moment would restore that lost splendor" (21). Perhaps the most famous example is Hemingway's short story "Big Two-Hearted River," in which a war-weary Nick Adams returns to a favorite trout stream on Michigan's Upper Peninsula to calm his soul.

The Big Two-Hearted River was also an important place for the teenage Peacock. In *Grizzly Years* he recounts his first long solo backpack trip there, and the spirit of Hemingway's story pervades the book. After the war, Peacock, like Nick Adams, returns to his favorite wild places, in his case the canyons of the Colorado Plateau and the alpine lakes of the Wind River range in Wyoming. Like Nick, he camps and goes fishing. But there the similarity ends. For unlike Nick Adams, Peacock remained enraged, aggressive, rude, physically ill, depressed, not a little paranoid, and "armed to the teeth with a .22 Magnum derringer of Saturday night manufacture, .357 and .44 Magnum Ruger single-action handguns, plus a bolt-action .30 = 06 rifle and a 12-gauge Ithaca Lefever double-barreled shotgun." As if this is not enough, he also carries "a complement of more primitive weapons."[3]

Peacock is plagued by memories of Vietnam and presents them in a clean prose reminiscent of Michael Herr's Vietnam classic *Dispatches.* At the same time, he loves wild nature, sensing, correctly, that the wild will free him from his anguish. But how? Camping and fishing do not go far enough. The cure must be equal to the terror of its origin, and camping and fishing are not Vietnam.

Just what might be required is hinted at near the end of "Big Two-Hearted River" when Nick reaches a cedar swamp and decides not to continue. He reacts against wading "in fast deep water, in the half light." Then an odd note: "In the swamp fishing was a tragic adventure. Nick did not want it" (198). This turn away from risk keeps Hemingway's story at the level of sport, just as Hemingway's own relation to nature remained at the level of sport. The prose mirrors the timid narrative. The threshold at which Hemingway's literal description would prove inadequate to experience—the point at which myth and nonlinguistic practices would be required to communicate—is the point where Nick, and Hemingway, turn back. Peacock went on into the metaphorical wild swamp. This is the second reason for his importance.

Grizzly Years transmits a message about wildness that is difficult to communicate. It differs from most contemporary nature writing. Peacock lacks the sheer mastery of Barry Lopez and Peter Matthiessen, the scientific inclination of David Quammen and Gary Nabhan. He moves too much to ground his writing in the sense of place that marks the work of John Hay, John Haines, or Wendell Berry. He is not a poet like Gary Snyder, he is not *primarily* a writer, like, say Annie Dillard. What, exactly, is Peacock?

In his introduction to *Words From the Land,* Stephen Trimble interviews some of our finest nature writers. The result is surprising. Many deny they are environmentalists or naturalists, much less inhabitants of wilderness. They are, they say, first and foremost, writers. Annie Dillard admits, "I distrust the forest, or any wilderness, as a place to live." And in her fine book, *The Writing Life,* she says, "The writer studies literature, not the world" (68).

Trimble's interviews reveal how much our love of nature has become a bookish love and how rare it is, even among nature writers, to find someone whose primary study is the physical world. How many nature writers walk Thoreau's four hours a day, or wander the wild for years like Muir, or spend several months a year in the presence of a wild animal like a grizzly bear? Not many. This is the worm in the rose of nature writing, for there is little reason to believe the wild earth will be preserved by writers with little experience of wildness and wilderness.

At its best, this bookishness elaborates other important traditions. Wendell Berry's 100-page essay "Poetry and Place" produced 187 footnotes. Ann Zwinger's *A Desert Country Near the Sea* lists hundreds of references. This prodigious scholarship presupposes the 2,500-year-old traditions grounded in the typologies of Aristotle and the hexameters of Hesiod, traditions that provide rich sources of reference, allusion, apprehension, response, and authority. Wendell Berry can echo Virgil, Ann Zwinger can echo Pliny. Whom does Peacock echo?

There are no footnotes or references in *Grizzly Years,* no books for Peacock to call upon for authority. The experts on the natural history of grizzly bears are not necessarily experts on how to "get along" with grizzlies. The people capable of teaching Peacock about grizzlies are gone, and they did not produce books. He tells us that the Blackfeet, the only tribe that truly respected the grizzly (calling them "Real Bear"), vanished before they could transmit their wisdom, and many of the tribes that remain match our ignorance and greed toward the natural world. What Peacock required was a context, but he was be-wild-ered, lost, not in space, but in mind; lacking not direction, but a usable tradition. *Grizzly Years* and Peacock are *sui generis*—one of a kind.

Edward Hoagland wrote that "Henry David Thoreau lived to write, but Muir lived to hike."[4] Peacock is like Muir. He writes well and his film footage is magnificent, but one feels that for him, as for Muir, the experience, not the writing, was primary. *Grizzly Years* carries within it an injunction: "Get out there, make contact." It is a defense of a *kind* of experience, one that only a few nature writers have shared.[5] Nothing is more endangered than experience of the wild, and Peacock's defense of wild experience is the third reason he is important.

How can we express this experience, especially in the absence of a rich tradition? Confronted with the wild near the summit of Maine's Mt. Katahdin, Thoreau's uncommonly acute powers of physical description were replaced by Milton and Greek mythology, and Thoreau thought myth was the most appropriate literary form to express what he called the wild.[6] *Walden* is his myth, perhaps our only modern myth of the wild.

Faulkner would have agreed. The section of *Go Down, Moses* called "The Bear" is a myth, the one most relevant to Peacock's experience with grizzlies. In "The Bear," the wilderness of swamp and forest dies, the bear, Old Ben, dies, the wild dog Lion, who brings Old Ben to bay, dies, and with their deaths, Sam Fathers, the old half-blood Chickasaw Indian, dies. Their deaths are honored by ritual. There is a tin box containing "Old Ben's dried mutilated paw, resting above Lion's bones" and another box nailed to a tree that the young boy Ike McCaslin fills with "the twist of tobacco, the new bandanna handkerchief, a small paper sack of the pepper-mint candy which Sam had used to love" (312–13). The vehicle of meaning here is not language but a practice, in this case what would now be called shamanic practice, which Faulkner perhaps knew from Chickasaw religion or black voodoo culture.

Grizzly Years opens in Yellowstone National Park with a ritual that is clarified in the remainder of the book. Peacock honors a bear killed by a sheepherder. He honors her spirit by returning her skull to her den. "Moving quickly, I set the skull on the framework of woven willow facing the den. I slipped a small bear paw of silver and turquoise off my neck and draped it over the skull; your fur against the cold, bear. When my skull lies with yours will you sing for me?" (11). We also learn he has "brought together a ghost herd of bison skulls, decorated with feathers of crane and eagle, the re-cipients of bundles of sage and handfuls of earth carried in from sacred mountains and offered up in private ceremonies" (82). And at the end of the book, we find he has constructed a cairn on a remote ridge in the Piedras Negras Wilderness, a monument "to those I had loved and lost." It contains skulls, feathers, arrowheads, shards, pieces of white shell, candles, and some paper. When he visits this wild memorial, he feels each object carefully, lying them one by one in the sun. Then he adds some new items from his pack and sits cross-legged and mourns.

This is not a common use of national parks and wilderness areas. Some, no doubt, will disapprove. But I believe these rituals are important attempts to fill a void in our traditions, an attempt to integrate the wild and the self by myth. The influence is American Indian—Chickasaw, early Sioux scaffold burials and Assinibboin medicine signs painted by Karl Bodmer,[7] the personal decoration of the Crow and Blackfeet—but it is *just* influence: Peacock is try-ing to figure something out for himself.

Peacock is not a shaman; he lacks that tradition and he's too wise to think he can simply give it to himself. But he made contact with the forces that drive shamanism, and these forces are expressed by a mixture of the self and wildness. His attempt to integrate the wild and the self without a tradition simply magnifies our loss of these traditions, and his difficulty is an omen: it registers the complexity of myth-making under conditions of modernity.

In "The Bear," Faulkner has the older McCaslin explain the loss of the wild by evoking some of the most beautiful lines in the English language: "She cannot fade, though thou hast not thy bliss / Forever wilt thou love, and she be fair."[8] The young McCaslin says, "He's talking about a girl." But the older McCaslin explains, "He was talking about truth. Truth is one. It doesn't change. It covers all things which touch the heart—honor and pride and pity and justice and courage and love . . . and what the heart holds to becomes truth, as far as we know truth" (283–84).

One does not kill, destroy, or exploit what one truly loves. Neither Sam Fathers nor young Ike McCaslin could kill Old Ben, though both had the chance. "He did not move, holding the useless gun which he knew now he would never fire at it, now or ever" (194). In *Grizzly Years*, Peacock reaches the same point of not killing. His memoir raises the possibility that we might still, at this late moment, hold a predator—the ultimate Other—to our heart, might actually come to love its wild and utterly different life, might actually achieve a unity. I believe the preservation of wilderness and wildness in all it forms depends upon this possibility.

The bear, the gun, the possibility of killing, the decision to limit one's power, the urge to honor the spirits of the Other—all these are present in *Grizzly Years* when Peacock begins to heal.

Peacock's journey led him to Yellowstone, a place with "magic." He needed isolation and wildness, and this soon led to grizzly bears. In his first terrifying contact with a grizzly he found something greater than himself, a redeemer who is not a god but an omnivore at the top of the food chain. A self-willed predator fully equal to the terror of war. The grizzlies give him an experience of wildness that breaches ordinary experience and brings Peacock to the edge of epiphany:

> The big bear stopped thirty feet in front of me. I slowly worked my hand into my bag and gradually pulled out the Magnum. I peered down the gun barrel into the dull red eyes of the huge grizzly. He gnashed his jaws and lowered his ears. The hair on his hump stood up. We stared at each other for what might have been seconds but felt like hours. I knew once again that I was not going to pull the trigger.

My shooting days were over. I lowered the pistol. The giant bear flicked his ears and looked off to the side. I took a step backward and turned my head toward the trees. I felt something pass between us. The grizzly slowly turned away from me with grace and dignity and swung into the timber at the end of the meadow. . . . I felt my life had been touched by enormous power and mystery. (61)

Confronted with a grizzly, Peacock — "a trained killer" — finds restraint. The not-killing opens his heart and, as Faulkner suggests, gives him access to the wild realm. The bear bestows a gift from the bear realm to the human realm, a gift Peacock reciprocates when he returns the bear's skull to her den. These practices re-create a web of interconnection with the natural world that we have lost. They immerse the self so deeply in the wild that boundaries of self and Other dissolve. This identification of self and wild carries *Grizzly Years* beyond the therapeutic jive of most nature writing into a possible landscape of reciprocity and redemption. This fusion of restraint and merger with wild animals creates a different kind of self and is the fourth reason for Peacock's importance.

The restoration of wilderness is a fad that, for many reasons, I do not believe will work. But we can restore our relation to wildness, for "wild" names the quality of a relationship, one in which we are not in control.

To restore is to reestablish a prior condition. Restoration is a *return* to a past state, conceived as normal or healthy, that preceded the current corruption. Contact with this state is deemed therapeutic and healing — Thoreau's tonic. We return from the wild more capable of coping with the burdens of what Charles Taylor calls "ordinary life" — our fundamentally Puritan focus on work and family at the expense of nearly everything else.[9] Perhaps most of our love of wild nature is explained by this tonic, but there are other possibilities.

Redemption requires more than restoration; it requires an exchange. When we redeem, we give; in return, we receive — nickels for coupons, cash for stocks, salvation for our sins. Thus, Christ was the Redeemer. Redemption leads to freedom and transcendence, to a higher state, not a return to a former state. Redemption is not about our ego and psychotherapy but about an anguish in the soul.

Grizzly Years is a religious text, a chronicle of a religious transformation of the self using wild nature. It is filled with the language of love and the spiritual. Peacock says he was on "a larger quest of some kind." The bear he faces commanded "awe," and the "muscular act of grace" when the grizzly grants him quarter is described as a "transcendence." The result is salvation: "These bears had saved my life" (67).

What follows are years of "Zen-like days" of careful observation indexed to visits with particular bears—part of a pilgrimage, another religious practice. "My year begins when I see the Bitter Creek Griz in April; then I see Happy Bear at Glacier in the summer, the great Black Grizzly at the Grizzly Hilton, also in Glacier in autumn, and then the strange Blond Grizzly I first saw the same day a woman was fatally mauled ten miles east at Many Glacier. In late October I drop back down from the Glacier Park area into Yellowstone" (95).

By repeatedly making pilgrimages, Peacock achieves an intimacy with particular grizzlies. They become individuals. The facts of their lives allow Peacock to present information about their natural history, biology, behavior, and their place in myth. Many books on bears describe the genus *Ursus arctos horribilis,* its history and behavior, but *Grizzly Years* inverts this abstract emphasis with an intimate and personal account that strongly suggests that tonics, cures, redemption, and salvation arise from long-term contact with particular wild creatures, not with an abstract concern for preservation, conservation, ecological integrity, or ecosystems management. The potential of this inversion is the fifth reason for Peacock's importance.

As Peacock opens his heart to the grizzlies, there are close calls and humorous mistakes, but he continues to survive because his manners, as a guest in the wild, are impeccable, a detailed study of how to treat wild animals as something more than entertainment. This, in turn, has consequences for how he views wilderness. He doesn't treat wilderness as a piece of federal property.

At one point he exclaims, "The entire concept of wilderness as a place beyond the constraints of culture and human society was itself up for grabs" (65). *Up for grabs!* What a wonderful attitude, enough to make postmodernists apoplectic. At a time when some environmental philosophers are trying to convince us there is no such thing as wilderness, Peacock is trying to figure out what to do with what is left.

Our federal institutions have done everything they can to assure that the concept of wilderness is not up for grabs and that intimate relations between wildlife and humans will not occur. The rhetoric of preservation implies separation: we belong here, the grizzlies belong there. With this separation the National Park Service and the Forest Service — always with our welfare and the welfare of wild animals and wild places in mind — prevent precisely the kind of experience that assumed fundamental importance not only in Peacock's life, but in the lives of Thoreau, Muir, Leopold, Marshall, and Murie.

Until now the preservation movement has primarily addressed issues of species and acreage. Although these remain important, they are not the only issues and, unfortunately, those concerned with preserving wilderness — from John Wesley Powell to David Brower and Dave Foreman — provide little guidance on its appropriate "use." Some are even appalled by such a notion. Their concern is preservation, not use. Indeed, except for the mildest forms of recreation and scientific investigation, they oppose use. Wilderness is a refuge for biodiversity, a collection of nice scenery, a playpen where we can escape our trying lives.

All this was explicit in the language of the Wilderness Act. The purpose of wilderness, according to the act, was "to secure . . . an enduring resource of wilderness . . . devoted to the public purposes of recreation, scenic, scientific, educational, conservation and historical use." In retrospect, one wonders why anyone believed that wilderness devoted to those public purposes would long remain wilderness. One wonders why anyone believed those public purposes encompassed what Thoreau and Muir were talking about. Indeed, the list ignores precisely what was most important to them: the human spirit and its experience of the wild.

Grizzly Years forces us to question what *our* appropriate use of wilderness is. It doesn't just tell us about grizzlies, it suggests a model of interaction appropriate to their wildness. Although Peacock is devoted to the preservation of the grizzly, he also *used* the wilderness and grizzlies. His experience suggests that wilderness will be usable as religious and mythic space only if we transcend one set of structures and practices with another set of structures and practices. Preservation and scientific study are merely infrastructure for the important work to come—the years of work to establish a relationship between ourselves and grizzlies, one that approaches in richness and reciprocity the relation between the Juwa Bushman and the African lion.[10]

We have a long, long way to go. In the autumn of 1994 a hunter armed with a .375 Holland & Holland magnum rifle—a powerful weapon usually used on African game—shot and wounded a grizzly while hunting in the Teton Wilderness Area in Jackson Hole, Wyoming. The grizzly still managed to maul him and was later killed by authorities. The man sued the Wyoming Game and Fish Department for a million dollars on the grounds that the state knew or should have known that the grizzly bear "was dangerous and likely to cause damage and injuries," yet "no precautions were taken." This in a wilderness area. His wife sued for another quarter million.[11]

Because our culture lacks traditions appropriate to Peacock's experience, *Grizzly Years* ends on an unhappy note. This is not Peacock's fault. As the book chronicles Peacock's life, a wild world of mast and corm and the signatures of individual bears gives way to a world of television talk shows, lecture circuits, and books. The primacy of raw experience shifts to the primacy of recording raw experience. Records can be sold, a living made. The result is desperation. "The man living with grace in the wilderness was an utter fuckup at home. I once imagined that the acquired ease with which I lived my life in the deserts and mountains might be transferred holistically to more domestic corners of my life. Apparently not" (286–87).

Indeed. Myths do not pay bills.

Returning a grizzly's skull to her den, being startled by a breaching whale, discovering a stone horse intaglio on the desert floor, hearing the deep silence of mountains—the potency of such experience will not easily translate into postmodern life. We hunger for a kind of experience deep enough to change our selves, our form of life. We realize that our ecological crisis is not, *at the roots,* caused by industrialization, capitalism, and technology, but by a particular form of the human self. We perceive, dimly, that preservation will have to alter this particular self, its greed, hate, fear, ignorance, and seemingly infinite desire for control. But in the context of postmodern culture, that will take courage, and courage is the rarest of virtues.

Peacock had the courage to transform his self in ways I do not fully understand. I do understand that he is stranded by his transformation. In this he is not unique, as Paul Zweig suggests in his study *The Adventurer.*

> Like the shaman, the adventurer crosses over into the mythic realm and returns with the story of his journey. By extruding his humanity beyond the frontier of human events, he embodies a victory over the visible world. For this he is condemned to a life of endless mobility. Because he is at home everywhere, he will be at home nowhere. His existence will be humanly pointless. The gods are angry with him, for he is a thief; men distrust him, because he is not entirely one of them. This is the sort of man Odysseus is: a danger to himself and to everyone he knows, a bringer of trouble, yet a figure worthy of epic, for he brings the knowledge which men need. He is a great storyteller too, because stories are his bond to the human world. Only they are able to vanquish the distance which his character secretes around him. He enthralls his audience, while remaining separate from them, expressed but also hidden by the tale he tells. (32–33)

Unfortunately, Peacock can no longer tell his story by the campfire, point over the ridge, and say, "Beware when you go there; there you will meet the Bitter Creek Griz. If so, take care; this is what I experienced." Gifts move by use and reciprocity. The elder gives, describing carefully; the apprentice receives, listening carefully—for tomorrow he may confront the Bitter Creek Griz.

These fires are gone now. Instead of apprentices, Peacock has a readership, an audience, strangers disembedded from the world of grizzlies, indeed, disembedded from the natural world and the wild creatures we insist must be preserved. But his story is still powerful for the same reason all well-told stories are powerful. As Walter Benjamin remarks in his essay "The Storyteller," "The value of information does not survive the moment in which it was new. It lives only at that moment; it has to surrender to it completely and explain itself to it without losing any time. A story is different. It does not expend itself. It preserves and concentrates its strength and is capable of releasing it even after a long time. . . . It resembles the seeds of grain which have lain for centuries in the chambers of the pyramids shut up air-tight and have retained their germinative power to this day" (90).

Peacock's story is a story with strength. It suggests that survival of the grizzly and a human teaching of the grizzly will develop together—or we will lose the grizzly. The necessary work of science produces information, but what we need are stories, stories that produce lore. *Grizzly Years* begins a modern lore of grizzly bears. This is my last reason for Peacock's importance.

Peacock is important because he managed to love large dangerous predators, to accept their wildness on its own terms, to defend his experience with them as important and curative, to merge with them psychologically and spiritually, to demonstrate the importance of intimacy with individual bears, and to begin a modern lore for the grizzly. This, alone, is an achievement. To write about it with emotion and intelligence is a considerable achievement. We should honor his odd and singular triumph, and take heart from his courage, so that our own lives may be rendered bolder by his victory.

8

Wildness and the Defense of Nature

Whatever part the whip has touched is
thenceforth palsied. — Henry Thoreau

Thoreau began talking about wildness as the preservation of the world in a lecture he gave at the Concord Lyceum on April 23, 1851, entitled "The Wild." In June of the following year he combined it with another lecture on walking and published the two as the essay "Walking, or the Wild" in the *Atlantic Monthly*. This essay remains the most radical document in the history of our conservation ethic, and as the distinguished Thoreau scholar Robert Richardson has so aptly put it, "how we understand that ethic depends on what we think Thoreau meant by 'wildness.'"[1]

Thoreau understood wildness as a quality: wild nature, wild men, wild friends, wild dreams, wild house cats, and wild literature. He associated it with other qualities: the good, the holy, the free. Indeed, he equated it with life itself. By freedom he meant not rights and liberties, but the autonomous and self-willed; and by life, not mere existence, but vitality and life-force. These connotations are not restricted to our culture. Gary Nabhan has noted that "the O'odham term for wildness, *doajkam,* is etymologically tied to terms for health, wholeness, and liveliness."[2]

Thoreau's famous saying "in Wildness is the preservation of the World" asserts that wildness preserves, not that we must preserve wildness. For Thoreau, wildness was a given; his task was to touch it and express it, and he believed myth expressed it best. His success was due not to political action or scientific study, but personal effort. As much as anything, the wild was a project of the self.

After Thoreau, the focus of our conservation ethic mutated from wildness to the preservation of wilderness, to habitat and species, and, recently, to biodiversity. This shift was broadly materialist, a move from quality to quantity, to acreage, species, and physical relations. The privileged status in our culture of classical science and its technologies virtually entailed this materialism, for classical science and its mathematics could not describe qualities like wildness, and what cannot be described is ignored. Wildness as quality, and its relation to other qualities, are now rarely discussed, the notable exception being Gary Snyder's *The Practice of the Wild.*

The shift was also reductive. By preserving things—acreage, species, and natural processes—we believed we could preserve a quality. Alas, collections of acreage, species, and processes, however large or diverse, no more preserve wildness than large and diverse collections of sacred objects preserve the sacred. The wild and the sacred are simply not the kinds of things that can be collected. Historical forms of access and expression can be preserved, but one cannot put a quality in a museum. At the same time, wildness cannot disappear. It can be diminished, in nature and in human experience, but it cannot cease to exist. The world contains many things that exist but cannot be collected and put someplace—the set of complex numbers, gravity, dreams. Wildness is similar and we are not very clear about how to preserve it.

There are excellent reasons to preserve wilderness, biotic communities, and biodiversity apart from any relation to wildness, reasons that are thoroughly covered in our environmental literature, but these materialist and reductive shifts in our conservation ethic have diminished the wildness of the places, species, and processes we have managed to preserve by diminishing their autonomy and vitality. Unfortunately, our conservation ethic tends to ignore this loss.

This diminution will continue because our efforts at preservation—parks, wilderness, zoos, botanical gardens—are conceived in terms of modern institutions, primarily the laboratory and museum, institutions that oppose autonomy and vitality. In the past, political and aesthetic criteria selected the samples; in the future (one hopes) biological and ecological criteria will be foremost. But no matter how large the selection, the processes of selection and implementation render the samples artificial. The environments (and their occupants) are selected and managed according to human goals—the preservation of scenery, of resources, of wilderness, of biodiversity. Our artifice fundamentally alters their order, extracting them from the larger context of interconnectedness that created that order. As Anthony Giddens says in discussing the consequences of modernity, "The 'end of nature' means that the natural world has become in large part a 'created environment' consisting of humanly structured systems whose motive power and dynamics derive from socially organized knowledge-claims rather than from influences exogenous to human activity."[3] This is just as true of national parks and designer wilderness as it is of Disneyland.

Created environments have that aura of hyperreality so common in modern life. They "are all updated forms of Cain's desire to return home by remaking the original creation. The tragedy is that in attempting to recover paradise we accelerate the murder of nature."[4] Nature "ends" because it loses its own self-ordering structure, hence its autonomy, hence its wildness.

Created environments also reek of the "museal" quality made famous by Theodor Adorno's essay "Valery Proust Museum": "The German word 'museal' [museumlike] has unpleasant overtones. It describes objects to which the observer no longer has a vital relationship and which are in the process of dying" (175). Just as cultural museums "testify to the neutralization of culture" (175), so I believe museums of land types, however diverse in habitat and species, testify to the neutralization of nature.

A created environment is a neutered wild, and a wild to which we no longer live in vital relationship. Museum objects may be useful, entertaining, and informative, and nature as laboratory may produce whole disciplines of new knowledge, but their subjects have lost their own organizing principles and are accurately described as relics — things left behind after destruction or decay of the original and preserved as objects of veneration.

In this sense it is possible to see the Earth as increasingly museal — in the process of becoming a relic; a once autonomous order transformed by a single species for its own use, a species that out of a combination of mourning and respect preserves bits and pieces for worship, study, and entertainment. The few pieces of remaining wilderness have long been valued as a laboratory — hence the title of Aldo Leopold's seminal essay "Wilderness as a Land Laboratory."[5] Stressed nature becomes another interesting scientific experiment, a problem to be solved, not unlike a sick patient, the chronically unemployed, a broken machine. Instead of a collection of gods (as for the Greeks), or the source of the Sublime (as for Kant and the Romantics), or a wellspring of moral instruction (as for Emerson, Thoreau, and Muir), nature turns subordinate to humans—dependent. A patient. Then, its philanthropic sensibilities aroused by crisis, Lord Man rushes to help the poor thing recover with GPS systems, computer databases, refuges, gene banks, and radio collars.

Recently we have discovered that our museums of land types are too small, disconnected, and artificial to allow species to maintain their own structure and order. Our remedy for these island ecosystems and relic populations is to create bigger and better created environments according to new theories, more data, and better management practices. This may lead to more complete ecosystems, and may sustain some species, but the increased human influence and the control mechanisms required for selection and preservation simultaneously diminish the ecosystem's self-organization and wildness. The relic "wilderness" becomes less and less natural as it submits to the management necessary for its survival, and, ironically, becomes less and less capable of fulfilling its purported scientific purpose—to serve as a benchmark for natural processes against which the health of man's trammeled world might be measured.

An example of this process can be found in the Wildlands Project proposed by Wild Earth: "a wilderness recovery program for North America" (which makes it sound like AA for the planet). If successful, it would become the world's largest created environment. Its order and structure—the cores, corridors, buffers, and dense-population areas—would undoubtedly be visible from space. I think of it as North America designed by Foreman, Noss, and Associates.[6]

Many feel the pervasive Disneyesque and museumlike quality of wilderness areas, national parks, and wildlife preserves, but they continue to believe these places provide a sanctuary from human artifice. This has always been an illusion. The national parks process millions of humans at the cost of natural processes. The "wilderness" of the Wilderness Act permits the state to control fire, insects, diseases, and animal populations; build trails for human use; graze livestock; and mine ore. These environments are not wild—they are too known, designed, administered, managed, and controlled to be wild.

All this suggests we need to imagine a new conservation ethic based on wildness. What we would come to mean by "wildness" could evolve from current interdisciplinary efforts by feminists, mathematicians, philosophers, and physicists to understand control, prediction, dominance, and their opposites: autonomy, self-organization, self-ordering, and autopoiesis.[7]

In his "Fact-Book," Thoreau noted that "wild" is the past participle of "to will": self-willed. A new wilderness ethic would highlight Thoreau's reference and confirm recent scholarship that interprets "wilderness" in its original sense of "self-willed land."[8] It would give teeth to the most important word in the most important passage in the Wilderness Act: "untrammeled." And finally, it would promote Thoreau's project of understanding the wild within us and within nature as fundamentally the same by their association, conceptually, with vitality and freedom.

I I

To construct a new conservation ethic, we need first to understand why we impose a human order on nonhuman orders. We do so for gain, the gain being in prediction, efficiency, and, hence, control. Faced with the accelerating destruction of ecosystems and the extinction of species, we believe our only option lies in increased prediction, efficiency, and control. So we fight to preserve ecosystems and species, and we accept their diminished wildness. This wins the fight but loses the war, and in the process we simply stop talking about wildness.

There are many ways we do this. For instance, we begin to substitute "wilderness" for "wildness," as in Thoreau's commonly misquoted saying "In *wilderness* is the preservation of the world."[9] But most (all?) of our designated Wilderness Act–wilderness is not wild. Take, for example, the Gila Wilderness, which is a pasture, not self-willed land. Thoreau did not claim that in ranching is the preservation of the world.

We also tend to equate wildness with biodiversity. For example, chapter 2 of Roger DiSilvestro's *Reclaiming the Last Wild Places: A New Agenda for Biodiversity* is entitled "Biodiversity: Saving Wildness," and there are phrases like "wildness in nature, which is what we preserve when we protect biodiversity" and "protection of biodiversity, of wildness" (25). But wildness is not biodiversity. Indeed, wildness may be inversely correlated with biodiversity. In *The Desert Smells Like Rain*, Gary Nabhan describes two oases.

The oasis occupied by the Papagos had twice as many bird species as the "wild" one preserved in Organ Pipe National Monument.[10] Neither oasis is wild in any meaningful sense of the term, and more remote and wilder desert oases might very well contain even fewer species. If so, so what? Is wildness less important than biodiversity? Should we preserve the latter at the cost of the former? What criteria would we use to decide the issue?

For many conservation biologists (though not, of course, for Nabhan) the important distinction is between "in the wild" and "in captivity," with "in the wild" now meaning a managed ecosystem. But if grizzlies are controlled in wilderness with radio collars and relocation policies, then what was for Thoreau the central question — freedom — simply drops out of the discourse on preservation.

We also ignore wildness when we define wilderness in terms of human absence. In "Aldo Leopold's Metaphor," J. Baird Callicott points out that with the exception of Antarctica, there has been no land mass without human presence, and therefore the wilderness of the Wilderness Act is an "incoherent" idea (45). Other people deny the existence of wildness on the grounds that any human influence on a species or an ecosystem destroys wildness, and since human influence has been around a long time . . . again, no wildness. This is absurd, and one wonders what Lewis and Clark, standing on the banks of the Missouri, would have thought of such talk. "This isn't wilderness. Why, there are millions of humans out there. And it isn't wild, either. Human influence has been mucking up this place for 10,000 years."

Something is wrong here, and I believe it can be traced to the fact that most people writing and thinking about wilderness issues know only Wilderness Act–wilderness. A week in the Amazon, the high Arctic, or the northern side of the western Himalayas would suggest that what counts as wildness and wilderness is determined not by the absence of people, but by the relationship between people and place. A place is wild when its order is created according to its own principles of organization — when it is self-willed land. Native peoples usually (though definitely not always) "fit" that order, influencing it but not controlling it, though probably not from a superior set of values but because they lack the technical means. Control increases with civilization, and modern civilization, being largely about control — an ideology of control projected onto the entire world—must control or deny wildness. This prospect is most clearly represented by the dystopian novels, beginning with Yevgeny Zamyatin's *We*.

Although autonomy is often confused with radical separation and complete independence, the autonomy of systems (and, I would argue, human freedom) is strengthened by interconnectedness, elaborate iteration, and feedback—that is, influence. Indeed, these processes create that possibility of change without which there is no freedom. Determinism and autonomy are as inseparable as the multiple aspects of a gestalt drawing.

The important point is that whatever kind of autonomy is in question—human freedom, self-willed land, self-ordering systems, self-organizing systems, autopoiesis—all are incompatible with external control. To take wildness seriously is to take the issue of control seriously, and because the disciplines of applied biology do not take the issue of control seriously, they are littered with paradoxes—"wildlife management," "wilderness management," "managing for change," "managing natural systems," "mimicking natural disturbance"—what we might call the paradoxes of autonomy. Collections of paradoxes are usually bad news for scientific paradigms, and I think the biological sciences face a major revolution.[11]

III

The biological sciences have played an increasingly imperial role in the conservation ethic since the days of Aldo Leopold. If the goal is to preserve ecosystems and species, then one goes to the experts: ecologists and biologists. During the past twenty years it has become obvious that the individual disciplines of applied biology were insufficiently comprehensive to achieve preservationist goals, especially biodiversity, and that they needed to be integrated with the newer disciplines of population biology and ecology—thus conservation biology. Conservation biology is an increasingly dominant voice for preservation in this country, if not the world, and the large environmental organizations that once led the fight for preservation often follow its agenda.[12]

Unfortunately, conservation biology is also about control. It integrates the controls already available in the biological, physical, and social sciences, which leads to what we might describe as meta-management. Since biodiversity is *understood* on the model of a scarce resource, the preservation of biodiversity becomes a problem *like* resource management.[13] In the face of biodiversity loss (and there surely is such a crisis), conservation biology demands that we do something, now, in the only way that counts as doing something—more money, more research, more technology, more information, more acreage. Trust science, trust technology, trust experts; they know best. In short, the prescription for the malady is even more control.

This mirrors the mode of crisis response familiar from Michel Foucault's studies of insanity, crime, and disease. Like psychiatry, criminology, and clinical medicine, conservation biology is a theoretical discipline that seeks control in pursuit of a morally pure mission: to end a crisis. Although the maladies addressed by these disciplines have always been with us (and have been handled by other cultures in more imaginative ways), they are exacerbated by the conditions of modernity—overpopulation, urbanization, and pathological social structures—and by the globalization of these conditions.

Unfortunately, instead of striking at causes, modern theoretical disciplines such as conservation biology strive to control symptoms. Their controls are directed at the Other, not at our own social pathologies. This mirrors the distinction between preventive medicine and intrusive medicine: instead of remaking ourselves and our societies, modern theoretical disciplines set about remaking the nonhuman world and diminishing its autonomy. Over the long term, this tends toward failure as the world resists and adapts to our intrusions, and as we, in turn, discover the true cost of our attempts at control.

These controls are always disciplinary or protodisciplinary in nature, and the multiple meanings of "discipline" here are not accidental. They involve capturing (shooting, darting, netting, trapping, apprehending, arresting), isolating in special areas (wards, prisons, refuges, wilderness), numerical identification (tattooing and tagging everything from inmates and soldiers to swans and grizzlies); technological representation (photography, X-rays, GPS mapping); chemical manipulation (of germs, of the brain, of fertility); surgery (lobotomies for the mad, and for predators, the implantation of radio transmitters or radioactive plaques to make their feces visible from satellites); monitoring (radio collars on animals, ankle monitors on prisoners, heart monitors for cardiac patients) — and constant surveillance to accumulate ever more information. Having severely intruded upon the human body and mind, we now intend to intrude upon the rest of creation, thus confirming the forecast in Ecclesiastes: "For that which befalleth the sons of men befalleth beasts."

Justified in the name of normality and equilibrium — just as wars are justified by "peace in our time" — disciplinary technologies tend to develop into grand schemes of salvation: economics wars against poverty, criminology wars against crime. Despite pockets of success, these wars fail. Prisons create more criminals, and poverty and hunger increase under modern economies. Unfortunately, these failures neither debase the disciplines nor halt their wars. Like Avis, disciplinary technologies just try harder, that is, they try to control more and control better.

Conservation biology is in this tradition of grand salvation. It wants to conduct a war for biodiversity, thus its missions and strategies (from the Greek word for army — *stratos*) to remake the natural world according to its own vision. I predict it will fail for the same reason other disciplines fail: it does not strike at the causes of its chosen malady but remains therapeutic. Its fondest hope is to arrest symptoms, and it presumes, desperately, that the malady is acute, not chronic.

True change comes from alteration of structure, not the treatment of symptoms. The structure that a radical ("root") environmental position must change is the positive-feedback system comprising overpopulation, urbanization, outrageously high standards of living, outrageously unjust distribution of basic goods; the conjunction of classical science, technology, the state, and market economics that supports the high standard of living; the endless presumptions concerning our rights, liberties, and privileges; and the utter absence of a spiritual life that might mitigate against these forms of greed. In short, the preservation of wildness, wilderness, and biodiversity requires a revolution against social pathology, a transformation of Western civilization — and let's face it, most of us turn chicken in the face of the challenge. We prefer to control nature.

In ecology, the most powerful statement of a conservation ethic of controlling nature is Daniel B. Botkin's *Discordant Harmonies: A New Ecology for the Twenty-First Century*. Botkin presents graphic evidence of the devastation caused by unmanaged elephants in

Tsavo, one of Kenya's largest national parks. He argues trenchantly that our current ideas about nature are outmoded, he calls for more management, more information, more monitoring, more research, more funding for education on the environment. He argues for the preservation of wilderness primarily as a baseline for scientific measurement. It is a powerful book. He concludes that "Nature in the twenty-first century will be a nature that we make; the question is the degree to which this molding will be intentional or unintentional, desirable or undesirable" (193).

Botkin is not alone. In an essay entitled "The Social Siege of Nature," Michael Soulé, one of the founders of conservation biology, says,

> Some of the ecological myths discussed here contain, either explicitly or implicitly, the idea that nature is self-regulating and capable of caring for itself. This notion leads to the theory of management known as benign neglect — nature will do fine, thank you, if human beings just leave it alone. Indeed, a century ago, a hands-off policy was the best policy. Now it is not. . . .
>
> Homeostasis, balance, and Gaia are dangerous models when applied at the wrong spatial and temporal scales. Even fifty years ago, neglect might have been the best medicine, but that was a world with a lot more big, unhumanized, connected spaces, a world with one-third the number of people, and a world largely unaffected by chain saws, bulldozers, pesticides, and exotic, weedy species.
>
> The alternative to neglect is active caring — in today's parlance, an affirmative approach to wildlands. (159–160)

Stewards of the cosmos? A nature that we make? This is the *reductio ad absurdum* of the American conservation movement. What used to be the goal of conservation — the preservation of the natural world and its own order — has been reduced to neglect, indeed, benign neglect, a term loaded with overtones of not caring. And the good side? Affirmative action — the usual liberal dodge. Disagree with conservation biology and you find yourself in the corner of *those who don't care about nature* because the debate has been framed in anthropocentric terms: what's the best medicine *we* can give to the poor old sick world? Soulé's Manichean management policy simply replays easy sixties rhetoric.

What does this mean for Thoreau's seemingly old-fashioned idea of wildness? The actual consequences of this management paradigm are clearly stated by David M. Graber, a research scientist with the National Biological Survey, in a discussion of management in national parks:

Parks are increasingly becoming ecological islands as the landscapes that surround them are converted to agriculture or development. Thus while climate change can be expected to lead to the local extirpation of species in parks, the invasions of many native "replacement" species — those adapted to the new climate — will be blocked by isolation. The intentional introduction or maintenance of native species could in some cases be used to facilitate the introduction of species that would have arrived on their own before habitat fragmentation, as well as to preserve the survival of other species that would no longer be sufficiently adapted to persist under the new climatic and ecological conditions. Such intensive management is in fact likely to be needed to preserve species of plants and animals that already are local in distribution.

To manage parks in this way emphatically abandons the contemporary ecologically based notion of wildness. We indeed become trapped into caring for the rest of life in a transformed world.[14]

This is indeed a dilemma. We wish to protect and preserve wild nature, but it appears that to do so we must accommodate a rather hard-nosed scientific positivism which in the biological sciences takes the form of an equally hard-nosed management style. The result of this management style is that we can save natural diversity only by destroying nature's own wild order. The alternative, "letting nature sort things out," is not seriously considered. Indeed it has become anathema, for even our pathetic attempts at control would be better than letting natural order rule the natural world.

These attitudes are about to become public policy. A recent volume of essays on ecosystem health suggests that "there exists considerable basis for expanding consensus if the concept of health is given its primary identity as a policy concept."[15] This removes the "health of nature" as a property of the world, reduces it to human policy, and, in turn, virtually insures that biologists and ecologists will go about fixing the world with treatments and remedial actions. That is the irony of Soulé's essay: he rues the social siege of nature but fails to see that the biological sciences are leading the charge, as though, somehow, biology and ecology are not part of the matrix of social construction.

Ecological management is Foucault's normalization and disciplinary control projected from social institutions onto ecosystems. The Otherness of the natural world is consumed by current social policy, and the new doctors of nature go about their mission— evangelists laboring once more amongst wild populations (now plants and animals instead of peoples) bringing the gift of modern order and our current version of salvation—the preservation of biodiversity.

This salvation implies trust in abstract systems, and since the lay person has neither the knowledge or ability to evaluate the foundations of these abstract systems, our trust is less a matter of knowledge than of faith. Those who are old-fashioned will place their trust in themselves and those they know instead of in abstract systems. Some will, of course, claim they are quite compatible, but in the last analysis they are not compatible: when push comes to shove, you must decide where to place your trust. Trust in abstract systems and experts disembeds our relations to nature from their proper context. This is precisely why so many of us will no longer place our trust in science: it ignores individual places, people, flora, and fauna.

I, for one, do not want to know about grizzlies in general, nor can I in any practical way care about grizzlies in general. I want to know and care about the grizzly that lives in the canyon above me. And I have more trust in myself, my friends, and that grizzly than I do in the managers sitting in universities a thousand miles away who have never seen this place or this grizzly and want all of it subsumed by a mathematical model.

IV

In this situation, one would like to believe that radical environmentalists can offer something different from what mainstream environmental organizations and conservation biology offer. Unfortunately, this is no longer obvious.

During the past five years conservation biology has extended its influence to radical environmentalism, inverting themes that once legitimized its radical content. The transformation of part of

Earth First! into Wild Earth was a movement from personal trust and confrontation to trust in abstractions and conciliation with technology. In this transition it gained new followers (and much financial support), and lost others. It certainly lost me. Whereas science, technology, and modernity were once part of the problem, now they are a large part of the solution, and I fear that the Wildlands Project may reduce Wild Earth—certainly one of our best radical environmental organizations—to the political arm of a scientific discipline.

But, again, the key issue is control and autonomy, not science. Recent issues of *Wild Earth* and *Conservation Biology* have run debates about the management of wilderness and wild systems, but they haven't penetrated to the heart of the problem. Writing in *Wild Earth*, Mike Seidman concluded his exchange by saying, "It seems that the depth of my critique of management went unnoticed." Seidman was being a gentleman, since the other side of the "debate" was an extended non sequitur.[16]

The autonomy of natural systems is the skeleton in the closet of our conservation ethic, and although it is recognized, no one is dealing honestly with the issue. The problem appears in many forms. It explains the growing discontent with our control of predators, the elk hunts in Grand Teton National Park, the slaughter of elephants for management, and the trapping and training of the last condors. It explains the increasing discontent surrounding the reintroduction of wolves to Yellowstone National Park. For a decade, environmentalists fought for an experimental population; now, faced with the biological and political control on that experimental population, many people would have preferred natural recovery—no matter how long it takes.

Biological controls are now ubiquitous. Biologists control grizzlies, they trap and radio-collar cranes, they have cute little radio backpacks for frogs, they bolt brightly colored plastic buttons to the beaks of harlequin ducks, they even put radio transmitters on minnows. And always for the same reason: more information for a better, healthier ecosystem. Information and control are indivisible, a point made in great detail by James R. Benninger in *The Control Revolution: Technological and Economic Origins of the Information Society*. It is the main point, perhaps the only point, of surveillance.

The great need, now, is to begin to imagine an alternative. Perhaps we don't need more information; maybe the emphasis on biological inventories, species recovery, surveillance, and monitoring is a further step in the wrong direction. And what could possibly be radical about all this? The Nature Conservancy has been doing it for years, and the Department of the Interior is going to do it too. Trying to be radical about, say, biological inventories is like trying to be radical about laundromats: it just isn't big enough, conceptually, to reach the source of the problem.

The radical environmentalist's obsession with roads and dams betrays a crude, industrial idea of destroying nature and blinds us to less visible modern control technologies that imply even more potent modes of destruction. But instead of a general critique of control we have deep ecologists like George Sessions and Arne Naess supporting, in principle or in practice, genetic engineering.[17]

Somehow the key issue is increasingly veiled by lesser issues. We need big wilderness, big natural habitat, not more technological information about big wilderness. Why not work to set aside vast areas where we limit all forms of human influence: no conservation strategies, no designer wilderness, no roads, no trails, no satellite surveillance, no over-flights with helicopters, no radio collars, no measuring devices, no photographs, no GPS data, no databases stuffed with the location of every draba of the summit of Mt. Moran, no guidebooks, no topographical maps. Let whatever habitat we can preserve go back to its own self-order as much as possible. Let wilderness again become a blank on our maps. Why don't the radical environmental organizations push for that? I suspect a large part of the answer is this: there is no money in it, and like all nonprofits, they need a lot of money just to survive, much less achieve a goal.

V

There are two senses of "preservation," and most preservationist efforts have followed the first: the preservation of things. Strawberry preserves epitomize this kind of preservation. The other sense is the preservation of process: leaving things be. Doug Peacock presents the second sense with great clarity, calling biology "Biofuck" and saying, "Leave the fucking bears alone."[18] This echoes Abbey's "Let being be," a quote from Heidegger, who stole it from Lao Tzu:

Do you want to improve the world?
I don't think it can be done.

The world is sacred.
It can't be improved.
If you tamper with it, you'll ruin it.
If you treat it like an object, you'll lose it.
. . . .
The Master sees things as they are,
without trying to control them.
She lets them go their own way,
and resides at the center of the circle.[19]

Although most of the public believes this is the preservation ethic, leaving things alone is definitely the new minority tradition among preservationists. But consider carefully the admonition that "If you tamper with it, you'll ruin it. / If you treat it like an object, you'll lose it." This goes to the heart of what I call "the abstract wild" — wildness objectified and filtered through concepts, theories, institutions, and technology.

What if the effect of scientific experts creating environments, treating ecosystems, and managing species is (sometimes, often, always?) as bad, or worse, than the effects of unmanaged nature? In short, leave aside the question of "Should we manage nature?" and ask "How well does (can) managing nature actually work?" Ecologists tend not to talk about this for fear of giving aid to the enemy, but the subject demands careful examination.

In an essay entitled "Down from the Pedestal: A New Role for Experts," David Ehrenfeld, for many years the editor of *Conservation Biology,* presents several examples of predictive failure in ecology and the unfortunate consequences for natural systems. Consider, for instance, the introduction of opossum shrimp into northwestern lakes with the purpose of increasing the production of kokanee salmon. "The story is complicated, involving nutrient loads, water levels, algae, various invertebrates, and lake trout, all interacting. But the bottom line is that the kokanee salmon population went way down rather than way up, and this in turn affected populations of bald eagles, various species of gulls and ducks, coyotes, minks, river otters, grizzly bears, and human visitors to Glacier National Park." Indeed, Ehrenfeld goes on to say that "biological complexity, with its myriad internal and external variables, with its open-endedness, pushes ecology and wildlife management a little closer to the economics . . . end of the range of expert reliability" (148–150).

Economics? Really? This from one of the deans of conservation biology? We are to entrust the management of nature to experts whose reliability is akin to economists? This removes a bit of the glitter from the remaking nature agenda, doesn't it? I wouldn't let them manage my front yard.

Ecologists are compared with economists because of their problems with prediction. Prediction (some think) is the essence of science: No prediction, no science; lousy prediction, lousy science. Unless (according to this view) the biological sciences can generate accurate, testable, quantitative predictions, they are well on their way to joining the dismal science of, say, astrology. Well, if your idea of good science requires quantitative prediction, particularly long-term quantitative predictions, then all the sciences are looking a bit dismal, ecology especially so.[20]

The historian of ecology Donald Worster, in his essay "The Ecology of Order and Chaos," notes that "Despite the obvious complexity of their subject matter, ecologists have been among the slowest to join the cross-disciplinary science of chaos" (168). This is not quite fair. Robert May, a mathematical ecologist at Oxford, is one of the pioneers of chaos theory, and his book *Stability and Complexity in Model Ecosystems* remains a classic. But Worster's point is still telling, and one suspects that the ecologists' lack of openness on the subject probably has something to do with the unsettling consequences for the practical application of their discipline—and hence their paychecks. They keep hanging on to the hope of better computer models and more information, but as Brecht said in another context, "If you're still smiling, you don't understand the news."

Most of the rapidly growing literature on chaos and complexity is either journalistic or extremely technical.[21] Of greater importance for radical thinking about the environment are the philosophical implications of chaos and complexity and their impact on those biological disciplines we depend on to guide environmental policy. An excellent examination of the former is in Stephen H. Kellert's *In the Wake of Chaos: Unpredictable Order in Dynamical Systems*, which suggests, as Ehrenfeld's examples suggest, that the problems facing the practical applications of ecology and biology are more formidable than the disciplines are willing to admit.[22] For the impact of chaos theory on ecological theory, required reading is Stuart L. Pimm, "Nonlinear Dynamics, Strange Attractors, and Chaos," in *The Balance of Nature? Ecological Issues in the Conservation of Species and Communities,* a sobering book for anyone who believes the issues are either understood or that we have sufficient empirical data to make intelligent decisions about long-term ecosystem management.

Many biologists and ecologists believe the autonomy of nature is a naive ideal, and that we must now attempt to control the Earth. Ironically, this view is widespread despite recent work in nonlinear dynamics that demonstrates nature's talent for self-organization, indeed its talent for organizing itself to critical states that collapse unpredictably with avalanches of the very events that so disturb us — earthquakes, wildfires, extinctions, epidemics. Indeed, many natural systems seem attracted to disequilibrium (or, I would say, wildness).[23] Some of the largest, most catastrophic events — like the Yellowstone fires in 1988 — are precisely the unpredictable events that are the key to forming the vegetation architecture basic to the order of an ecosystem. And yet these are the events we most wish to manage.

What emerges from the recent work on chaos and complexity is the final dismemberment of the metaphor of the world as machine, and the emergence of a new metaphor — a view of a world that is characterized by vitality and autonomy, one which is close to Thoreau's sense of wildness, a view that, of course, goes well beyond him, but one he would no doubt find glorious. Instead of a vast machine, much of nature turns out to be a collection of dynamic systems, rather like the mean eddy lines in Lava Falls, where the description of the turbulence is a nonlinear differential equation containing complex functions with "free" variables that prevent a (closed form) solution. Such natural systems are unstable; they never settle into equilibrium. (Kayakers know this in their bodies.) They are aperiodic; like the weather, they never repeat themselves but forever generate new changes, one of the most important of which is evolution. Life evolves at the edge of chaos, the area of maximum vitality and change.

Dynamic systems marked by chaos and complexity do have an order, and the order can be described mathematically. They are deterministic, and we can (usually) calculate probabilities and make qualitative predictions—how the system will behave *in general*. But with chaos and complexity, scientific knowledge is again limited in ways similar to the limits of incompleteness, uncertainty, and relativity.

That does not end science; all that drops out, really, is long-term quantitative prediction, and that affects most science primarily in one way: control. But that's the nut of the problem. As John Ralston Saul has said, "The essence of rational leadership is control justified by expertise." [24] Without control, there is no expertise. The biological sciences lose their leadership of the conservation ethic. The "preservation as management" tradition that began with Leopold is finished because there is little reason to trust the experts to make intelligent long-range decisions about nature.

What happens to the rationality of managing species and ecosystems without accurate prediction and control? If the microsystems of an ecosystem—from vascular flows to genetic drift to turbulence—plus all of the natural disturbances to ecosystems—weather, fire (the front of a wildfire is a fractal), wind, earthquakes, avalanches—if all these exhibit chaotic and/or complex behavior, and some organize themselves at a global level to critical states resulting in catastrophic events, and further, if such behavior does not allow long-term quantitative predictions, then isn't ecosystems management a bit of a sham? The management of grizzlies and wolves at best a travesty? If an ecosystem can't be known or controlled with scientific data, then why don't we simply can all the talk of ecosystem health and integrity and admit, honestly, that it's just public policy, not science?

Much of the best intellectual labor of this century has led to the admission of various limits in science and mathematics—of axiom systems, observation, objectivity, measurement. This should have a humbling effect on all of us, and the limits of our knowledge should define the limits of our practice. The biological sciences should draw the line of their operations at wilderness—core wilderness, Wilderness Act–wilderness, any wilderness—for the same reasons atomic scientists should accept limits on messing with the atom, and geneticists should accept limits on messing with the structure of DNA: *We are not that wise, nor can we be.*

The issue is not the legitimacy of science in general, nor the legitimacy of a particular scientific discipline, but the appropriate limits to be placed on any scientific discipline in light of limited knowledge. To ignore these limits is to refuse humility and undermine the foundations of the preservation movement. Accepting these limits and imagining a new conservation ethic based on wildness and humble, careful, non-intrusive practice would unite Thoreau's insight that "in Wildness is the preservation of the World" and the traditions of ancient wisdom with the intuitions of our most radical wilderness lovers, ecofeminists, and cutting-edge mathematicians and physicists. This is as consoling as it is charming.

All knowledge has its shadow. The advance of biological knowledge into what we call the natural world simultaneously advances the processes of normalization and control, forces that erode the wildness that arises from nature's own order, the very order that, presumably, is the point of preservation. At the core of the present conjunction of preservation and biological science—the heritage of Leopold—lies a contradiction. We face a choice, a choice that is fundamentally moral. To ignore it is mere cowardice. Shall we remake nature according to biological theory? Shall we accept the wild?

Wildness is out there. The most vital beings and systems hang out at the edge of wildness. The next time you howl in delight like a wolf, howl for unstable aperiodic behavior in deterministic non-linear dynamical systems. Lao Tzu and Thoreau and Abbey will be pleased.

Notes

1 The Maze and Aura

1 Schopenhauer, *The World as Will and Idea*, vol. 3, 145.
2 Benjamin, "The Work of Art," in *Illuminations*.
3 For a further discussion of aura, see Benjamin's essay "On Some Motifs in Baudelaire," also reprinted in *Illuminations*. Obviously, how these different qualities are affected by the loss of aura is complex. For instance, Benjamin says that the reproduction of a natural object does not affect its authenticity. But I think it is a matter of scale: the gross reproduction of the natural world affects the authenticity of the natural world.

2 The Abstract Wild: A Rant

1 Cover, *Wildlife Damage Review* (spring 1992).
2 See Berry, *The Unsettling of America.*
3 Adam Roberts, "The Uses of Civil Resistance."
4 Dōgen Zenji, "Upon Looking at Mr. Ran's Last Words," in *Moon in a Dewdrop*, 219.
5 Marx, "Theses on Feuerbach," 245.
6 Herbert Marcuse, *One Dimensional Man*, 9.
7 See Nabhan, *Enduring Seeds*, and Peacock, *Grizzly Years.*
8 Trow, *Within the Context of No Context.*
9 In *Travels in Hyperreality*. Eco's essay is one of the most important yet written on preservation—of animals, land, art. Its universe of the copy and the fake is central to any understanding of postmodernism. See also Baudrillard, "Simulacra and Simulations."
10 John Berger, "Why Look at Animals," 24.
11 Leopold, *A Sand County Almanac*, 224–25.
12 Associated Press, August 29, 1989.
13 Quoted in Cohen, *The Pathless Way*, 303.
14 Thoreau, "Ktaadn," in *The Maine Woods*, 71.

3 Mountain Lions

1. William Blake, "The Tiger."
2. Cover, *Wildlife Damage Review* (spring 1992).

4 Economic Nature

1. From Gerard Manley Hopkins' poem "Pied Beauty."
2. See Anthony Giddens, *The Consequences of Modernity.* Trust doesn't disappear, but its focus moves from kin and community to abstract systems, especially money and a culture of experts.
3. Bill Turque, "The War for the West," *Newsweek* 118, no. 14 (September 30, 1991): 18; Florence Williams, "Sagebrush Rebellion 2."
4. Paul Shepard describes this process in "Varieties of Nature Hating," chapter 7 of *Man in the Landscape.*
5. Quoted by Kemmis in *Community and the Politics of Place,* 20.
6. See Worster, *Under Western Skies;* Brown, *Bury My Heart at Wounded Knee;* Limerick, *The Legacy of Conquest;* and White, *It's Your Misfortune and None of My Own.*
7. Opening address at the 1991 Mont Pelerin Society meeting, Big Sky, Montana.
8. Quoted in Kenneth Lux's *Adam Smith's Mistake,* 202.
9. Quoted in Lux, 203.
10. Quoted in Evernden, *The Natural Alien,* 16.
11. Snyder, *No Nature,* 80.
12. Goodman, "The Way the World Is," 56.
13. Hyde, "Laying Waste to the Future."

5 The Song of the White Pelican

1. Quoted in Maezumi, *The Way of Everyday Life,* n.p.
2. Schaller, "Breeding Behavior of the White Pelican." Although it is somewhat dated, Schaller's article contains a bibliography of works on the white pelicans of Yellowstone Lake.
3. In Blythe, *Haiku,* vol. 4, 1259.
4. *Peacock's War,* Bullfrog Films, 1989.
5. Quoted in Krutch and Ericksson, *A Treasury of Birdlore,* 31.
6. Dōgen Zenji, *Moon in a Dewdrop,* 97.
7. Murie, *A Field Guide to Animal Tracks,* 96.

6 In Wildness Is the Preservation of the World

1. Kittredge, "What Do We Mean?"
2. See Sherman Paul, *The Shores of America,* 412–17, and Richardson, *Henry Thoreau,* 224–27.
3. Thoreau, "Walking," in *The Natural History Essays,* 130.
4. This is the meaning given by Eric Partridge in *Origins: A Short Etymological Dictionary of Modern English* (New York: Macmillan, 1958).
5. Gould, "Unenchanted Evening," *Natural History* (September 1991): 14.
6. Shepard, *Nature and Madness,* 132.
7. Translated by Lewis Hyde and used as an epigraph for his book *The Gift.*

7 The Importance of Peacock

1 Peacock, *Grizzly Years*, 243.
2 Ibid., 16.
3 Ibid., 17.
4 Hoagland, "In Praise of John Muir."
5 For other fine examples, see John Baker, *The Peregrine*, and Harley Shaw, *Soul Among Lions.*
6 See Thoreau, *The Maine Woods*, 64–71, and Richardson, *Henry Thoreau,* 230–33.
7 See the paintings in *Karl Bodmer's America* (Lincoln: Joslyn Art Museum and University of Nebraska Press, 1984).
8 From John Keats's "Ode on a Grecian Urn."
9 Taylor, "The Affirmation of Ordinary Life, part 3 of *The Sources of the Self.*
10 See Thomas, "The Old Way."
11 *Jackson Hole News*, February 1, 1995.

8 Wildness and the Defense of Nature

1 Richardson, *Henry Thoreau,* 225.
2 Nabhan, "Cultural Parallax in Viewing North American Habitats," in *Reinventing Nature*, eds. Michael Soule and Gary Lease (Washington, D.C.: Island Press, 1995).
3 Giddens, *Modernity and Self-Identity,* 144. See also his book *The Consequences of Modernity.*
4 Gary Coates, quoted in Jerry Mander, *In the Absence of the Sacred,* 149.
5 In Leopold, *The River of the Mother of God and Other Essays.*
6 See Reed F. Noss, "The Wildlands Project," 10–25.
7 Because of women's experience in being dominated, much of the best work on control has been done by feminists. See Susan Griffin's *Woman and Nature: The Roaring Inside Her* and Carolyn Merchant's *The Death of Nature.*

   Among the best discussions of autonomy is Evelyn Fox Keller, *Reflections on Gender and Science,* part 2, chapter 5. On autopoiesis, see Humberto R. Maturana and Francisco J. Varela, *Autopoiesis and Cognition* and *The Tree of Knowledge.* On self-organizing systems, see I. Prigogine and I. Stengers, *Order out of Chaos.*
8 For Thoreau's "Fact-Book" and a discussion of "wildness," see Sherman Paul, *The Shores of America,* 412–17. For a discussion of "wilderness" as "self-willed land," see Jay Hansford C. Vest, "Will of the Land."
9 Richard B. Primack committed this common error in *Essentials of Conservation Biology,* 13.
10 Nabhan, *The Desert Smells Like Rain,* chapter 7. See also Peter Sauer's introduction to *Finding Home.*
11 See Paul Hoyningen-Huene, *Reconstructing Scientific Revolutions,* on paradox in scientific theories.
12 See chapter 1 of Primack, *Essentials of Conservation Biology.*
13 See the diagram linking conservation biology and resource management in Primack, *Essentials of Conservation Biology,* 6.

14 Graber, "Resolute Biocentrism," 131.

15 Robert Costanza et al., *Ecosystem Health,* 14.

16 Mike Seidman's original letter appeared in *Wild Earth* 2 (fall 1992): 9–10. Responses to his letter by Reed F. Noss, W. S. Alverson, and D. M. Waller appeared in *Wild Earth* 2 (winter 1992/93): 8–10. Seidman's reply is in *Wild Earth* 3 (spring 1993): 7–8.

17 Salleh, "Class, Race, and Gender," 233.

18 Quoted in Rick Bass, "Grizzlies: Are They Out There?"

19 Lao Tzu, *Tao Te Ching,* chapter 29, trans. Stephen Mitchell. Mitchell deserves the Nobel Peace Prize for his use of the feminine pronoun.

20 For chaos and predictive failure in classical economics, see Richard H. Day, "The Emergence of Chaos from Classical Economic Growth."

21 The classic, of course, is James Gleick's *Chaos: Making A New Science.* See also M. Mitchell Waldrop, *Complexity: The Emerging Science at the Edge of Order and Chaos,* and Roger Lewin, *Complexity: Life at the Edge of Chaos.* The most accessible introduction to the technical issues is John Biggs and F. David Peat, *Turbulent Mirror.* For discussions of chaos in fields ranging from ecology to quantum physics. see Nina Hall (ed.), *Exploring Chaos: A Guide to the New Science of Disorder.*

22 For a general introduction to the problem of prediction see John L. Casti, *Searching For Certainty.*

23 See Per Bak and Kan Chen, "Self-Organized Criticality," and Per Bak, "Self-Organized Criticality and Gaia."

24 Saul, *Voltaire's Bastards,* 10.

Bibliography

✳

Adorno, Theodor. "Valery Proust Museum." In *Prisms*. Cambridge: MIT Press, 1986.

Bak, Per. "Self-Organized Criticality and Gaia." In *Thinking About Biology: An Invitation to Current Theoretical Biology*. Sante Fe Institute Studies in the Sciences of Complexity, Lecture Notes, vol. 3. New York: Addison-Wesley, 1993.

Bak, Per, and Kan Chen. "Self-Organized Criticality." *Scientific American*, January 1991.

Baker, John. *The Peregrine*. Moscow, Idaho: University of Idaho Press, 1967.

Bass, Rick. "Grizzlies: Are They Out There?" *Audubon* 95 (Sept.—Oct. 1993).

Baudrillard, Jean. "Simulacra and Simulations." In *Jean Baudrillard: Selected Writings*. Stanford, Calif.: Stanford University Press, 1988.

Benjamin, Walter. *Illuminations*. New York: Schocken Books, 1968.

Benninger, James R. *The Control Revolution: Technological and Economic Origins of the Information Society*. Cambridge, Mass.: Harvard University Press, 1986.

Bent, Arthur Cleveland. *Life Histories of North American Petrels and Pelicans and Their Allies*. New York: Dover, 1964.

Berger, John. "Why Look at Animals." In *About Looking*. New York: Pantheon Books, 1980.

Berry, Wendell. "Poetry and Place." In *Standing by Words*. San Francisco: North Point Press, 1983.

———. *The Unsettling of America: Culture and Agriculure*. San Francisco: Sierra Club Books, 1986.

Biggs, John, and F. David Peat. *Turbulent Mirror*. New York: Harper & Row, 1989.

Blythe, R. H. *Haiku*. Vol. 4. Toyoko: Hokuseido Press, 1982.

Bodmer, Karl. *Karl Bodmer's America*. Lincoln: Joslyn Art Museum and University of Nebraska Press, 1984.

Botkin, Daniel B. *Discordant Harmonies: A New Ecology for the Twenty-First Century.* New York: Oxford University Press, 1990.

Brown, Dee. *Bury My Heart at Wounded Knee.* New York: Henry Holt and Company, 1970.

Callicott, J. Baird. "Aldo Leopold's Metaphor." In *Ecosystem Health: New Goals for Environmental Management,* edited by Robert Costanza, Bryan G. Norton, and Benjamin D. Haskell. Washington, D.C.: Island Press, 1992.

Casti, John L. *Searching For Certainty.* New York: William Morrow and Company, 1990.

Castleton, Kenneth B. *Petroglyphs and Pictographs of Utah: The South, Central, West, and Northwest.* Vol. 2. Salt Lake City: Utah Museum of Natural History, 1979.

Cohen, Michael P. *The Pathless Way: John Muir and the American Wilderness.* Madison: University of Wisconsin Press, 1984.

Cole, Sally J. *Legacy on Stone: The Rock Art of the Colorado Plateau and the Four Corners Area.* Boulder, Colo.: Johnson Books, 1990.

Costanza, Robert, Bryan G. Norton, and Benjamin D. Haskell, eds. *Ecosystem Health: New Goals for Environmental Management.* Washington, D.C.: Island Press, 1992.

Day, Richard H. "The Emergence of Chaos from Classical Economic Growth." *Quarterly Journal of Economics,* May 1983.

Devall, Bill, and George Sessions. *Deep Ecology.* Salt Lake City, Utah: Peregrine Smith Books, 1985.

DeVoto, Bernard. *Across the Wide Missouri.* Boston: Houghton Mifflin, 1947.

Dillard, Annie. *The Writing Life.* New York: Harper & Row, 1989.

DiSilvestro, Roger L. *Reclaiming the Last Wild Places: A New Agenda for Biodiversity.* New York: John Wiley & Sons, 1993.

Dōgen Zenji. *Moon in a Dewdrop: Writings of Zen Master Dōgen.* Edited by Kazuaki Tanahashi. San Francisco: North Point Press, 1985.

Dunn, John. *The Political Thought of John Locke.* New York: Cambridge University Press, 1969.

Eco, Umberto. *Travels in Hyperreality.* New York: Harcourt Brace Jovanovich, 1986.

Ehrenfeld, David. "Down from the Pedestal: A New Role for Experts." In *Beginning Again: People and Nature in the New Millennium.* New York: Oxford University Press, 1993.

Evernden, Neil. *The Natural Alien.* Toronto: University of Toronto Press, 1993.

Faulkner, William. *Go Down, Moses.* New York: Vintage Books, 1940.

Feuer, Lewis S. *Marx and Engels: Basic Writings on Politics and Philosophy.* New York: Anchor Books, 1989.

Flader, Susan L., and J. Baird Callicott, eds. *The River of the Mother of God and Other Essays by Aldo Leopold.* Madison: University of Wisconsin Press, 1991.

Giddens, Anthony. *The Consequences of Modernity.* Stanford, Calif.: Stanford University Press, 1990.

————. *Modernity and Self-Identity.* Stanford, Calif.: Stanford University Press, 1991.

Gleick, James. *Chaos: Making a New Science.* New York: Penguin Books, 1987.

Goodman, Nelson. "The Way the World Is." In *The Review of Metaphysics* 14 (1960).

Graber, David M. "Resolute Biocentrism: The Dilemma of Wilderness in National Parks." In *Reinventing Nature.* Washington, D.C.: Island Press, 1995.

Griffin, Susan. *Woman and Nature: The Roaring Inside Her.* New York: Harper-Collins, 1979.

Grumbine, R. Edward. *Ghost Bears: Exploring the Biodiversity Crisis.* Washington, D.C.: Island Press, 1992.

Hall, Nina, ed. *Exploring Chaos: A Guide to the New Science of Disorder.* New York: W. W. Norton & Company, 1991.

Hemingway, Ernest. "Big Two-Hearted River." In *The Nick Adams Stories.* New York: Charles Scribner's Sons, 1972.

Herr, Michael. *Dispatches.* New York: Knopf, 1977.

Hoagland, Edward. "In Praise of John Muir." In *On Nature.* San Francisco: North Point Press, 1987.

Hoyningen-Huene, Paul. *Reconstructing Scientific Revolutions: Thomas S. Kuhn's Philosophy of Science.* Chicago: University of Chicago Press, 1993.

Hyde, Lewis. *The Gift: Imagination and the Erotic Life of Property.* New York: Random House, 1979.

———. "Laying Waste to the Future." *New York Times Book Review,* Sept. 27, 1987.

Jordon, William. "Pictures at a Scientific Exhibition." In *Divorce Among the Gulls: An Uncommon Look at Human Nature.* San Francisco: North Point Press, 1991.

Keller, Evelyn Fox. *Reflections on Gender and Science.* New Haven: Yale University Press, 1985.

Kellert, Stephen H. *In the Wake of Chaos: Unpredictable Order in Dynamical Systems.* Chicago: University of Chicago Press, 1993.

Kemmis, Daniel. *Community and the Politics of Place.* Norman: University of Oklahoma Press, 1990.

Kittredge, William. "What Do We Mean?" *Northern Lights* 6 (fall 1990).

Krutch, Joseph Wood, and Paul S. Eriksson, eds. *A Treasury of Birdlore.* New York: Doubleday & Company, 1962.

Lao Tzu. *Tao Te Ching.* Translated by Stephen Mitchell. New York: Harper-Collins, 1988.

Lawrence, T. E. *Seven Pillars of Wisdom.* New York: Doubleday & Company, 1935.

Leopold, Aldo. *The River of the Mother of God and Other Essays by Aldo Leopold.* Edited by Susan L. Flader and J. Baird Callicott. Madison: University of Wisconsin Press, 1991.

———. *A Sand County Almanac.* New York: Oxford University Press, 1949.

Lewin, Roger. *Complexity: Life at the Edge of Chaos.* New York: Macmillan, 1992.

Limerick, Patricia Nelson. *The Legacy of Conquest: The Unbroken Past of the American West.* New York: W. W. Norton, 1987.

Lux, Kenneth. *Adam Smith's Mistake*. Boston: Shambhala, 1990.

Maezumi, Hakuyu Taizan. *The Way of Everyday Life*. Los Angeles: Center Publications, 1978.

Mander, Jerry. *In the Absence of the Sacred: The Failure of Technology and the Survival of the Indian Nations*. San Francisco: Sierra Club Books, 1991.

Marcuse, Herbert. *One Dimensional Man: Studies in the Ideology of Advanced Industrial Society*. Boston: Beacon Press, 1964.

Marx, Karl. "Theses on Feurbach." In *Marx and Engels: Basic Writings on Politics and Phiolosophy*, edited by Lewis S. Feuer. New York: Anchor Books, 1989.

Maturana, Humberto R., and Francisco J. Varela. *Autopoiesis and Cognition*. Boston: D. Reidel, 1980.

———. *The Tree of Knowledge: The Biological Roots of Human Understanding*. Boston: Shambhala, 1992.

May, Robert M. *Stability and Complexity in Model Ecosystems*. Princeton, N.J.: Princeton University Press, 1973.

McMullen, James P. *Cry of the Panther*. Englewood, Fla.: Pineapple Press, 1984.

Merchant, Carolyn. *The Death of Nature*. San Francisco: Harper & Row, 1990.

Mitchell, Stephen, trans. *Tao Te Ching*. New York: HarperCollins, 1988.

Murie, Olaus. *A Field Guide to Animal Tracks*. Boston: Houghton Mifflin, 1974.

Nabhan, Gary. *The Desert Smells Like Rain*. San Francisco: North Point Press, 1982.

———. *Enduring Seeds*. San Francisco: North Point Press, 1989.

Noss, Reed F. "The Wildlands Project Land Conservation Strategy." *Wild Earth*, special issue.

Noss, Reed F., W. S. Alverson, and D. M. Waller. Letter. *Wild Earth* 2 (winter 1992–93).

Nozick, Robert. *The Examined Life*. New York: Simon and Schuster, 1990.

Ortega y Gasset, José. *Meditations on Hunting*. New York: Charles Scribner's Sons, 1972.

O'Toole, Randal. *Reforming the Forest Service*. Washington, D.C.: Island Press, 1988.

Palmer, R. S. *Handbook of North American Birds*. Vol. 1. New Haven, Conn.: Yale University Press, 1962.

Patterson, R. M. *The Dangerous River*. Post Mills, Vt.: Chelsea Green, 1990.

Paul, Sherman. *The Shores of America: Thoreau's Inward Exploration*. Urbana: University of Illinois Press, 1958.

Peacock, Doug. *Grizzly Years: In Search of the American Wilderness*. New York: Henry Holt and Company, 1990.

———. *Peacock's War*. Bullfrog Films, 1989.

Pimm, Stuart L. *The Balance of Nature? Ecological Issues in the Conservation of Species and Communities*. Chicago: University of Chicago Press, 1991.

Pollan, Michael. *Second Nature*. New York: Atlantic Monthly Press, 1991.

Power, Thomas Michael. *The Economic Pursuit of Quality*. Armonk, N.Y.: M. E. Sharp, 1988.

Prigogine, I., and I. Stengers. *Order out of Chaos*. New York: Bantam Books, 1984.

Primack, Richard B. *Essentials of Conservation Biology.* Sunderland, Mass.: Sinauer Associates, 1993.

Richardson, Robert D., Jr. *Henry Thoreau: A Life of the Mind.* Berkeley: University of California Press, 1986.

Roberts, Adam. "The Uses of Civil Resistance in International Relations." In *Violence and Aggression in the History of Ideas,* edited by Philip P. Wiener and John Fisher. New Brunswick, N.J.: Rutgers University Press, 1974.

Rothchild, Michael. *Bionomics: Economy as Ecosystem.* New York: Henry Holt and Company, 1992.

Salleh, Ariel. "Class, Race, and Gender Discourse in the Ecofeminism/Deep Ecology Debate." *Environmental Ethics* 15(3) (fall 1993).

Sauer, Peter, ed. *Finding Home.* Boston: Beacon Press, 1992.

Saul, John Ralston. *Voltaire's Bastards: The Dictatorship of Reason in the West.* New York: Random House, 1992.

Schaafsma, Polly. *The Rock Art of Utah.* Salt Lake City: University of Utah Press, 1994.

Schaller, George B. "Breeding Behavior of the White Pelican at Yellowstone Lake, Wyoming." *The Condor* 66(1) (1964).

Schopenhauer, Arthur. *The World as Will and Idea.* Translated by R. B. Haldane and J. Kemp. London: Routledge and Kegan Paul, 1983.

Seidman, Mike. Letter. *Wild Earth* 2 (fall 1992).

————. Letter. *Wild Earth* 3 (spring 1993).

Shaw, Harley. *Soul Among Lions: The Cougar as Peaceful Adversary.* Boulder, Colo.: Johnson Books, 1989.

Shepard, Paul. *Man in the Landscape: A Historic View of the Esthetics of Nature.* College Station: Texas A&M University Press, 1991.

————. *Nature and Madness.* San Francisco: Sierra Club Books, 1982.

Snyder, Gary. *No Nature: New and Selected Poems.* New York: Pantheon, 1992.

————. *The Practice of the Wild.* San Francisco: North Point Press, 1990.

Soulé, Michael. "The Social Siege of Nature." In *Reinventing Nature.* Washington, D.C.: Island Press, 1995.

Tanahashi, Kazuaki, ed. *Moon in a Dewdrop: Writings of Zen Master Dogen.* San Francisco: North Point Press, 1985.

Taylor, Charles. *The Sources of the Self.* Cambridge: Harvard University Press, 1989.

Thomas, Elizabeth Marshall. "The Old Way." *The New Yorker,* Oct. 15, 1990.

Thoreau, Henry David. *The Maine Woods.* Princeton, N.J.: Princeton University Press, 1972.

————. *The Natural History Essays.* Salt Lake City, Utah: Peregrine Smith Books, 1984.

Trimble, Stephen. *Words From the Land.* Salt Lake City, Utah: Peregrine Smith Books, 1988.

Trow, George W. *Within the Context of No Context.* Boston: Little, Brown and Company, 1978.

Vest, Jay Hansford C. "Will of the Land." *Environmental Review* (winter 1985).

Waldrop, M. Mitchell. *Complexity: The Emerging Science at the Edge of Order and Chaos.* New York: Simion and Schuster, 1992.

White, Richard. *It's Your Misfortune and None of My Own*. Norman: University of Oklahoma Press, 1993.

The Wilderness Society. *The National Wilderness Preservation System*. Washington, D.C.: The Wilderness Society, 1989.

Wilkinson, Charles F. *The Eagle Bird: Mapping a New West*. New York: Pantheon, 1992.

Williams, Florence. "Sagebrush Rebellion 2." *High Country News* 24(3) (Feb. 24, 1992).

Williams, Terry Tempest. *Refuge*. New York: Pantheon Books, 1991.

Worster, Donald. "The Ecology of Order and Chaos." In *The Wealth of Nature*. New York: Oxford University Press, 1993.

———. "Natural Questions: Chaos Theory Seeps into Ecology Debate Stirring Up a Tempest." *The Wall Street Journal*, July 11, 1994.

———. *Under Western Skies: Nature and History in the American West*. New York: Oxford University Press, 1992.

Young, Michael D. *The Metronomic Society: Natural Rhythms and Human Timetables*. Cambridge, Mass.: Harvard University Press, 1988.

Zamyatin, Yevgeny. *We*. New York: Penguin, 1993.

Zweig, Paul. *The Adventurer*. New York: Basic Books, 1974.

Zwinger, Ann. *A Desert Country Near the Sea*. Tucson: University of Arizona Press, 1987.

ABOUT THE AUTHOR

Jack Turner was educated at the University of Colorado and Cornell University, and he taught philosophy at the University of Illinois before leaving academia for a more adventurous life. Turner has been climbing for thirty-six years in Yosemite, Colorado, and the Tetons, and he has also led or participated in more than forty treks and expeditions to Pakistan, India, Nepal, Tibet, China, and Peru. In the winter, Turner lives on a remote ranch on the Mexican border, and in summer he lives in Grand Teton National Park, where he works for the Exum Guide Service and the School of American Mountaineering. His book on the Tetons will be published by Henry Holt.